I'M A CHRISTIAN NOW!

GROWING IN MY FAITH

90-DAY DEVOTIONAL JOURNAL
WITH DAILY ACTIVITIES

CONTRIBUTING EDITOR
PAT CONNER

LifeWay Press®
Nashville, TN 37234

ISBN 9781462740987

Item 005793051

DEWEY: 242.62

SUBHD: CHILDREN--RELIGIOUS LIFE \ DISCIPLESHIP \ REGENERATION (CHRISTIANITY)

Printed in the United States of America

Kids Ministry Publishing

LifeWay Church Resources

One LifeWay Plaza

Nashville, Tennessee 37234-0172

We believe the Bible has God for its author; salvation for its end;
and truth, without any mixture of error, for its matter
and that all Scripture is totally true and trustworthy.

To review LifeWay's doctrinal guideline,
please visit www.lifeway.com/doctrinalguideline.

All Scripture quotations are taken from the Christian Standard Bible®
Copyright 2017 by Holman Bible Publishers. Used by permission.

CONTENTS

I'M A CHRISTIAN, NOW!
Growing in My Faith Journal

Congratulations! By trusting in Jesus as Savior and Lord, you have become a member of God's family. Now that you are a Christian, it is important to learn what comes next. That is the purpose of this journal. God has a very important plan for you. The information on these pages will help you learn how to live your life to fulfill God's plan. Here are some helps on how to use your journal.

- Ask your parents to read page 5. They will be your partners as you use the journal.

- Together, read the family devotion at the beginning of each week. Then you can complete the six days of activities on your own. Work to complete one day's activities at a time.

- On the first day of each section, read the introduction and complete the devotion for Day 1.

- At the bottom of each family devotion, you will find a weekly memory verse. Write it down and try to learn to say it without looking.

- Each day, find the "Verse of the Day" passage in your Bible. Take a few minutes to read and think about the verse(s).

- When you can, challenge yourself to read more from your Bible by locating, reading, and thinking about the "Challenge" verses.

- Make notes, write, and draw in your journal. This is your journal, so take notes about what you learn, what you think, and how God speaks to you.

- Listen for God to speak to you each day. (You will learn more about how to hear God later.)

- Keep your journal in a safe place.

- Almost everyone will miss a day or days when working through the journal. That is OK! If it happens to you, just start again where you stopped.

- Ask your parents (or another adult) to help you if you do not understand something.

- Follow the prayer suggestions on each day's devotion. You can pray out loud or silently. (You will learn more about how to pray later.) When you pray, take time to listen to what God says to you.

- Take as long as you need each day to complete the activities. Some days will be faster than other days.

- Pay attention to what you read. As you work through your journal, you may think you already read some of the information in a previous study. You are CORRECT! Some of the information about living the Christian life relates to more than one area and is included more than one time.

 Look for this symbol at you work through your journal. This symbol means it's time for a "Parent Talk!" You have reached a place where it would be good for your parents to read and discuss the information with you. When you see a Parent Talk symbol, take your journal to your parents and ask them to find a time to discuss it with you.

Dear Parents,

Your child has taken the most important step in his life by trusting in Jesus as his Savior and Lord. As Christians, we spend our lives on earth learning to understand what is involved in our walk with Jesus. Now is the time for your child to begin learning and practicing that walk of obedience.

God instructs you, parents, to teach your child about Him (Deuteronomy 6:4-9). This *Growing in My Faith* journal is designed to help you lead your child to grow in her understanding of what God has planned for each Christian. The Bible shows us that God's plan is for us to become like Jesus. This transformation will not be complete in this life, but each growing Christian continues to obey God joyfully, becoming an imitator of Jesus (Ephesians 5:1-2; 2 Corinthians 3:18). This takes discipline, and that is what this journal is all about. Each week, a section of devotionals will help your child focus on an aspect of training to be like Jesus. Just as you have helped your child develop other healthy habits such as brushing her teeth, this journal can help your child develop healthy *spiritual* habits, also known as spiritual disciplines. Please encourage her in this.

Each devotional section consists of a family devotion and six daily devotions to complete. Begin on Monday by reading the family devotion and Day 1 devotion with your child. No devotions are included for Sundays. Use this as a time to worship together and reflect on what you've learned throughout the week.

Encourage your child to complete most of the daily journal pages independently if possible. Allow him to learn how to use his Bible, respond to questions, and pray. Be available and ready to help when he needs assistance. One of the most important things you can do is pray for your child regularly. It is a privilege for parents to share in the spiritual growth of their children.

 The journal includes a suggested Parent Talk each week. This provides regular opportunities for you and your child to have conversations about what God is teaching her. Look for the Parent Talk symbol or ask your child to let you know when she sees it. Enjoy your discussions and enjoy the wonderful process of watching your child grow spiritually!

WHAT IS GOD'S PLAN FOR ME?

Do you ever wonder if God has a plan for you? He does! Look outside. What do you see or hear? Do you see grass growing? Hear birds singing? God planned that. The very same God who planned the world and everything in it has a special plan for you. That's exciting, right?

What is that plan? We don't know every single part of it yet, but we do know one of the most important parts of God's plan for you is be like Jesus. This is God's plan for every Christian. Now that you are a Christian, God expects you to become more like Jesus.

How do we know this plan? The Bible tells us. In 2 Corinthians 3:18, we learn that we are being changed to be like Jesus: "We all... are looking as in a mirror at the glory of the Lord and are being transformed into the same image from glory to glory..."

It is happening right now! This is what God has always planned (Romans 8:29), and one day it will be real. 1 John 3:2 says that one day we will be exactly like Jesus!

So let's get started! Using this book will help you become more like Jesus. How does that happen? How do Christians become more like Jesus? Here are a few ways.

Christians become more like Jesus when:
- We know more about who God is.
- We want to spend time with God.
- We pray and read the Bible.
- We respect and serve other people.
- We worship God.

There are some other things that you will be able to add to this list as you use this book, but this will get you started thinking about how God's plan works.

Look at the list again. Some of the things in the list show *actions* (reading the Bible, serving) and some of the words show *attitudes* (respect, want to). Did you notice that? It's important because in God's plan, you will become like Jesus in your attitudes *and* your actions. Stop and think. How much are you like Jesus right now in your attitudes? What about your actions?

Are you like Jesus in the things you do? There are probably changes that need to be made in your actions and your thoughts. We all have ways we need to change.

There is good news, though. God loves you so much. He made sure you have ways to follow His plan. He helps you change. You made a great start by becoming a Christian. Now it is time to do the work God planned for you to do. Each day you will have the opportunity to practice making changes in your attitudes and actions to become more like Jesus. It is what God planned for you!

"Therefore, be imitators of God, as dearly loved children, and walk in love, as Christ also loved us and gave himself for us."
Ephesians 5:1-2a

DAY 1

HOW AM I GROWING?

Verse of the Day: 2 Corinthians 5:17

Challenge: Jeremiah 29:11

 DO IT First, write today's date at the top of this page. You will need it later!

	AS A BABY	NOW
My weight		
My height		
My hair color		
My favorite food		

Find a picture of you as a baby. What are some ways you have grown? What are some things that helped you to grow?

 PARENT Talk Just like your body is growing and changing, you also grow as a Christian. What are some things that can help you grow as a Christian?

 KNOW IT ☐ You know you are growing as a Christian when you become more like Jesus in your actions and attitudes.
☐ You grow as a Christian by making it a habit to read the Bible and pray.
☐ You grow as a Christian by doing the things God tells you to do.

 PRAY IT Ask God to show you how you can change and grow to be more like Jesus. Thank Him for His plan for your life.

GOD'S PLAN FOR ME

DAY 2

HOW DO I GET STRONGER?

Verse of the Day: 1 Timothy 4:8

Challenge: 1 Corinthians 9:24-27

 DO IT Have you ever watched the Olympics? Follow the path for each sport equipment and write the name of the Olympic event it is used.

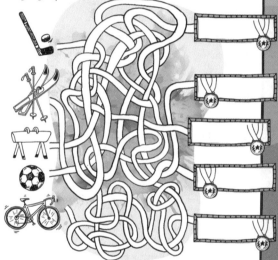

How do the Olympic athletes get ready to compete? They practice! Every day they are training to be stronger and better at their sport. Growing as a Christian is the same way. We have to train and practice every day to be more like Jesus.

 KNOW IT ☐ Getting stronger takes work.
☐ Spending time with God every day helps you grow as a Christian.
☐ Christians are training for the prize of being like Jesus.
☐ God will help you become like Jesus.

 PRAY IT Tell God you want to change to become more like Jesus. Ask Him to help you work toward this goal and to give you everything you need.

DAY 3
WHO DO I ADMIRE?

Verse of the Day: Romans 12:10

Challenge: Colossians 3:12-15

 DO IT Think of a friend (not Jesus) whom you admire. It could be an adult or another kid. It could be someone in your neighborhood or at school or anyone you would hope to be more like. In the box below, draw a picture of that person.

Around the picture you drew, write some of the qualities you admire about that person. Look at the qualities you list. Are those qualities that Jesus has? If they are, it shows you are already wanting to be more like Jesus!

 PARENT Talk Share the picture you drew with your parents. Talk about someone they admired as a kid and why. Discuss some of the qualities you both admire in others and how that points to Jesus.

 KNOW IT ☐ God brings people into our lives to help us know more about Him.
☐ Part of God's plan is that we would learn from other people how to be like Jesus.
☐ It is very important that we spend time with people who help us be like Jesus.
☐ We can learn what is important to us by understanding what we admire in other people.

 PRAY IT Thank God for the friend whose picture you drew. Ask God if the qualities you admire are pleasing to Him and if He will help develop those qualities in you.

DAY 4
WHAT IS JESUS LIKE?

Verse of the Day: 2 Peter 3:18

Challenge: Colossians 1:15-20

 DO IT Read the list of words below. If a word describes Jesus, circle it. If a word does NOT describe Jesus, put an X through it.

GENTLE

GOOD   STRONG

PEACEFUL

WISE

FAITHFUL   JOYFUL

KIND   LOVING

UNSELFISH   PATIENT

OBEDIENT

Did you find words that describe Jesus? All of them do! That's because Jesus is exactly who His Father, God, wants Him to be. The plan for you to become like Jesus is a plan for all of these things to become true of you too.

Has anyone ever told you that you look like someone? Maybe you look like one of your parents, a sibling, or someone famous! As we become like Jesus, we may not physically look like Jesus, but we do start to show His character qualities. That is good news!

 KNOW IT ☐ One of the reasons Jesus came to earth is to help us see what we should be like.
☐ God loves you so much, and He is helping you become like Jesus right now.
☐ Jesus is our example in all things.

 PRAY IT Thank God for the example of Jesus. Tell Him specific ways you want to be more like Him. Ask God to help you as you grow. He will help develop those qualities in you.

DAY 5
CHECK MY CHOICES

Verse of the Day: Philippians 2:5

Challenge: Romans 12:1-2

DO IT Think about some things that have happened to you this week. Write down three of them in the chart below. Every time something happens, you make a choice of how to respond. Were your responses like Jesus or not? Be honest. No one will see this but you. The first line is filled in as an example.

WHAT HAPPENED	HOW I RESPONDED	LIKE JESUS	NOT LIKE JESUS
Seth shoved me	Shoved back	☐	☑
Lily made fun of me	Said kind words	☑	☐
_____	_____	☐	☐
_____	_____	☐	☐
_____	_____	☐	☐

Look back at how you filled in the chart. It isn't always easy to take an honest look at ourselves. Could you think of times you did not respond like Jesus?

KNOW IT ☐ Every day we make many choices of how to respond in all kinds of situations.
☐ It's important to look back over our responses and check ourselves.
☐ It takes practice to become more like Jesus and to respond like He would.
☐ When we don't respond like Jesus, we need to ask His forgiveness and do better next time.

PRAY IT Ask God to make you aware of the way you respond every day and to show you when your attitudes or actions need to change.

DAY 6
KEEP GOING AND GROWING

Verse of the Day: Galatians 6:9

Challenge: Psalm 37:23-24

DO IT Can you find your way through this maze from start to finish? Don't go across any lines!

START

FINISH

Could you do it? Did you have to turn back and go a different way at all? Growing as a Christian is like that. We know what our goal is. We are growing as Christians to become more like Jesus, but sometimes we hit a wall or some obstacle. Don't forget that God wants us to keep going so we can keep growing!

KNOW IT ☐ When we make mistakes as Christians, God forgives us when we repent.
☐ He can and will still use those mistakes to help us grow.
☐ All Christians sin and make mistakes sometimes. When we ask Him, God forgives us.
☐ When you have trusted in Jesus, you are a Christian from now on. That can never change. God wants you to keep growing.

PRAY IT Thank God for loving us even when we get tired or make mistakes. Ask Him to help you keep growing no matter what.

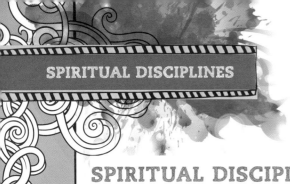

SPIRITUAL DISCIPLINES

You might think of "discipline" as a bad thing, like a punishment, but discipline actually means training. Just like athletes have to practice and train to be good at their sports, Christians have things we need to practice regularly to help us become more like Jesus. Those things are sometimes called "spiritual disciplines."

Look at each of the spiritual disciplines described on these pages. With each one, think about how much you are doing these things right now. Some of them you may do regularly, and some of them you may not do at all yet. That's OK. This is just for you to think about how you can grow.

Do this beside each of the spiritual disciplines described:

If it is something you do REGULARLY, draw a star.

If it is something you do sometimes, draw a circle.

If it is something you don't do yet, draw a triangle.

PRAYER

Talk and listen to God.

BIBLE STUDY

Read, study, and memorize God's Word.

WORSHIP

Praise God, focus on Him.

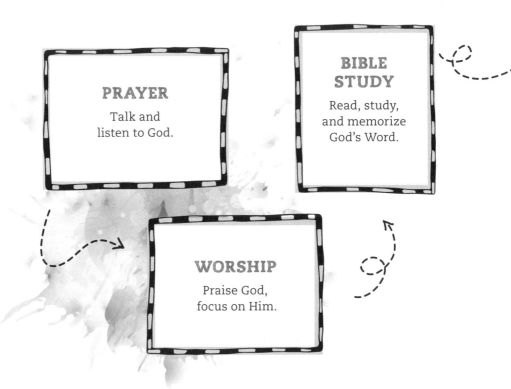

SERVICE

Become a servant to all.

SOLITUDE (ANOTHER WORD FOR ALONE)

Spend quiet time alone with God.

SUBMISSION

Give love, care, and respect to others.

GUIDANCE

Learn to know God's direction.

FASTING

Give up something for a while to focus on God (sometimes this can be giving up food, but not always).

GIVING

Know that everything we have belongs to God and gladly give back at least a tenth.

CONFESSION

Tell the truth about myself and about Jesus.

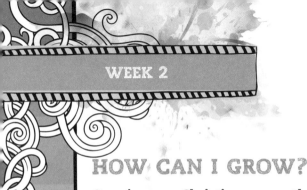

HOW CAN I GROW?

Growing as a Christian means that you have to get to know God better. How does that happen? Think of a few of your friends. How did you get to know them? It was probably by talking to them, listening to them, and spending time with them. That is exactly how you will get to know God better. He wants you to spend time with Him.

Spending time with God can happen any time. One way to be sure you grow as a Christian is by setting aside a special time every day to spend time alone with God. This special time with God is sometimes called a quiet time. A quiet time is a time to read your Bible, think about God, journal your thoughts, and pray.

Can a person really get to know God? Can a person talk to God? Can God hear when someone speaks to Him? The answer to all these questions is YES! God wants you to know Him. He wants you to be His friend. He wants you to become more like Jesus.

All of these things happen when you spend time studying the Bible and praying. Those are the best ways to get to know God better. Here are some things to think about.

God loves you. God knows everything about you and He loves you more than you can imagine. He wants you to know everything about Him, too.

God wants to spend time with you every day. How would you feel if you planned to spend time with your best friend after school, but your friend didn't show up? You might think you are not important to your friend. That would not feel good at all. When you make the effort to spend time alone with God, it shows that He is important to you.

The Bible helps you know more about God. The Bible is a book about God, and it was written for you. It shows you how Jesus lived His life. He always knew what God wanted Him to do and He always did it. Following His example is a way you can train to be like Jesus, and you can learn all about it in the Bible.

Prayer is an important way to grow in your friendship with God. What if you had a friend that you never talked to or listened to? That friendship would not be a very good one, would it? God wants you to talk to Him. He wants to talk to you. Prayer is the way to talk to and hear from God. Sometimes it takes practice for prayer to feel natural, but it is worth it!

This week you will learn more about how to have daily time with God. Decide right now to set aside some time each day to spend time with God. You will be glad you did!

"But grow in the grace and knowledge of our Lord and Savior Jesus Christ. To him be the glory both now and to the day of eternity." 2 Peter 3:18

DAY 1
THE THREE P'S

Verse of the Day: Psalm 1:2

Challenge: Psalm 1

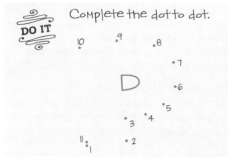

DO IT — Complete the dot to dot.

What letter did you discover? Let the letter P help you remember three things about your time alone with God.

PRIORITY is something that is very important. Is having time alone with God important to you?

Spending time with God helps you grow in your relationship with God.

PREPARATION is getting ready for something. Here's some help on getting ready.
→ Set an alarm to remind you.
→ Place your Bible, pencil, and journal in the same place so you can find it every day.
→ Open your Bible to bookmark tomorrow's verses after finishing today's study.

PLAN what you will do. Practice now!
→ Begin with a simple prayer such as, "God, help me learn about You today."
→ Read the day's verses.
→ Write down what God is teaching you.
→ Pray, asking God to help you apply what you learned to your life.

KNOW IT
☐ The Bible is true.
☐ The Bible is God's message.
☐ The Bible tells what Jesus is like.
☐ The Bible helps you understand how God wants you to live.

PRAY IT — Ask God to help you follow the 3 P's and grow in your relationship with Him.

DAY 2
WHERE WILL I BE?

Verse of the Day: Matthew 6:6

Challenge: Matthew 6:5-8

DO IT — Complete the "Quiet Place" activities on pages 16-17.

STOP what you are doing. Find a quiet place to talk to God. Tell God what you are thinking and feeling.

LISTEN to God as He speaks to you. Read and think about the words of Matthew 6:6. Ask God to help you hear Him.

LOOK around you. What can you thank God for today? Draw a picture of what you are thankful for.

KNOW IT
☐ God is everywhere at all times.
☐ God wants you to communicate with Him through praying and reading the Bible.
☐ God hears and answers prayers.
☐ God will speak to you through the Bible.

PRAY IT — Thank God for wanting to have a relationship with you. Ask Him to help you make it a priority to spend time with Him each day.

DAY 3
WHEN WILL I SPEND TIME WITH GOD?

Verse of the Day: Psalm 57:2

Challenge: Psalm 57:7-11

 DO IT Look at the clocks and the activities below. Draw a line from the activity to the clock showing the time closest to when you do that activity.

WAKING UP

EATING LUNCH

GETTING OUT OF SCHOOL

GOING TO BED

Things that are habits often happen around the same time every day. It's a good idea to plan a time for you to spend time with God in His Word and praying each day.

It doesn't have to be an exact time, but around the same time each day. What do you think? What would be a good time for you? Write that time here._____

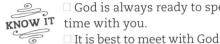 **KNOW IT**
☐ God is always ready to spend time with you.
☐ It is best to meet with God when you are not distracted by other things.
☐ Some people like to have quiet time in the morning and some like it later in the day. There is no right or wrong way to spend time with God.

 PRAY IT Tell God you want to meet with Him every day. Thank Him for always being ready to spend time with you.

PARENT Talk Time for a Parent Talk! Tell your parents when and where you think your regular time you will spend with God will be. Ask them what they think.

DAY 4
WHAT WILL I NEED?

Verse of the Day: Psalm 119:11

Challenge: Psalm 119:9-16

 DO IT What do you take with you when you go to school? What do you take when you go to someone's house for a sleepover? It's important to plan ahead. Around the backpack below, draw the things you think you will need for your time alone with God.

What did you draw? Did you draw a picture of a Bible? You will need this for sure! How about something you write with? After you finish this journal, you will keep spending time alone with God. It will always be good to have something to write in. It helps you remember what you learn.

 KNOW IT
☐ You can take your Bible with you wherever you go.
☐ Planning ahead for what you need shows that your time with God is important to you.
☐ Writing down your thoughts during this time helps you to focus.

 PRAY IT Thank God for giving you the chance to spend time with Him. Ask Him to help you plan and prepare for your time with Him.

DAY 5
WHAT WILL I DO?

Verse of the Day: Psalm 119:34

Challenge: Psalm 119:33-40

 DO IT Find the words READ, WRITE, THINK, PRAY, LEARN and STUDY in the puzzle below. Circle each word as you find it.

```
F  W  L  A  Y  T
L  R  E  A  D  H
P  R  A  Y  U  I
Z  T  R  B  T  N
V  E  N  M  S  K
P  W  R  I  T  E
```

Did you find all the words? Time you spend with God can look different for different people. Some people like to have music as part of their alone time with God. Some people like to listen to recorded Bible verses. For sure you will need to read the Bible and pray every time. That's how you learn more about God.

 KNOW IT ☐ God gave us the Bible so we can know Him better.
☐ God gave us the Bible so we can know how much He loves us.
☐ God gave us the Bible so we can learn how to be more like Jesus.

 PRAY IT Ask God to teach you things He wants you to know. Thank Him for loving you enough to spend time with you.

DAY 6
DON'T GIVE UP!

Verse of the Day: Jeremiah 33:3

Challenge: Joshua 1:1-9

 DO IT How would your best friends feel if you did not talk to them for several days? Write what you think your friends would feel here.

Ask your parents if you can call a family member you have not talked to in several weeks. After the call, think about these questions. How did the person respond? Was she excited to hear from you? What did you talk about? What did you learn from your family member?

How do you think God feels when you go several days without talking to Him?

 KNOW IT ☐ God wants you to spend time with Him every day.
☐ You can spend time with God anywhere and at any time. He is always ready to listen to you.
☐ The more you develop the habit of having time alone to pray with God and read your Bible, the easier it is to continue.

 PRAY IT Ask God to help you not to give up if you miss time with Him. Thank Him that you can talk to Him and read your Bible anytime and anywhere.

WHERE CAN I SPEND TIME ALONE WITH GOD?

Use the code box to discover 10 places you can spend time alone with God.

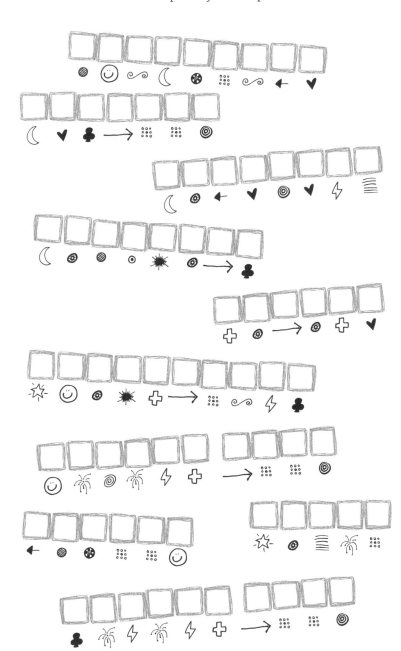

16

WHERE IS THE BEST PLACE FOR ME TO SPEND TIME ALONE WITH GOD?

THINK ABOUT THESE THINGS AS YOU DECIDE:

- Where is a quiet place so I can focus on what I am learning?

_____

_____

_____

- Where is a place private enough so I can read, write, and listen to God without someone interrupting me?

_____

_____

_____

- Is there somewhere I can go every day?

_____

_____

_____

- Would any of the places I discovered in the puzzle be good for me to spend time alone with God?

_____

_____

_____

- The place I will spend time alone with God will be...

_____

_____

_____

- I will spend time alone with God at _____ time each day.

_____

_____

WHY IS THE BIBLE SUCH A BIG DEAL?

Since books began being printed, there have been over 138 million books published. That is a lot! Of all these books, the Bible is the most amazing book ever. No other book can compare with the Bible. This week you will learn some of the reasons why.

It is important to know that God Himself wrote the Bible. No, He did not write down the actual words. He told ordinary men what words to write, and they did. For thousands of years people have studied the Bible. What was true when God told people what to write in the Bible is still true today. How do you know if the teachings of the Bible are true? Here are some things to think about.

→ The Bible itself makes the claim to be true (Psalm 119:160; 2 Timothy 3:16).

→ Jesus taught that the Bible is true and important (Matthew 4:1-11).

→ The Bible is historically correct. The names of many of the Roman officials in the Bible have been confirmed (proven to be correct) by ancient historical records and archaeology (a science that deals with past human life and activities).

→ Bible prophecies continue to come true. Jesus Himself fulfilled over 300 prophecies made several hundred years before He was born (Isaiah 7:14; 9:6).

→ The Bible has been taken care of and passed down through the generations of time. The Bible is very old, and has not changed through thousands of years.

→ The whole Bible points to Jesus and continues to change lives.

What can we learn from the Bible? There are so many wonderful things in the Bible. None of us will ever be able to understand and learn every single thing in this amazing book. It is also true that ordinary people, including kids, can read and understand many things God wants us to learn in the Bible. Here are a few things the Bible teaches us.

- The way God created our universe
- God's story of Himself
- God's rules people should follow
- The story of God's people
- The great gift God gave us in Jesus
- How to be a part of God's family
- How to live in relationship with God
- How to treat other people

This week's devotions will help you understand how amazing the Bible really is. As you are reading and studying, remember that the Holy Spirit will help you understand the Bible. When you read the Bible, you are actually connecting to God and what He wants to tell you.

"I have treasured your word in my heart so that I may not sin against you." Psalm 119:11

DAY 1
THE BIBLE IS GOD'S WORD

Verses of the Day: 2 Timothy 3:16-17

Challenge: Nehemiah 8:1-3

 DO IT Use the code box to discover five ways people communicate with one another.

B5 C1 B3 C1 C4 C2 B4 A4 C1

B5 C1 C5 B5

C3 C1 A5 A5 A1 B2 A3 A4 B2

A2 A1 B1 C1   B5 B4

A2 A1 B1 C1

C3 A1 A3 B3

A4 B4 B5 C1 A5

C1 C3 A1 A3 B3

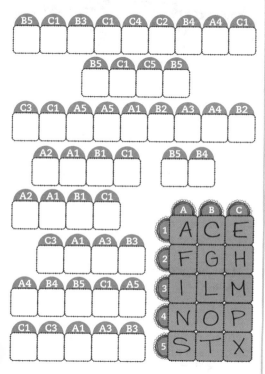

	A	B	C
1	A	C	E
2	F	G	H
3	I	L	M
4	N	O	P
5	S	T	X

What other ways do people communicate?

 KNOW IT ☐ God communicates in a variety of ways (prayer, people, thoughts, and the Bible).
☐ God inspired (told people) what to write in the Bible (1 Thessalonians 2:13).
☐ The Bible is God's message about Himself. It is perfect and trustworthy (Psalm 19:7).
☐ The Bible is the *only* written Word of God (Psalm 119: 89-90).

 PRAY IT Thank God for the Bible. Ask Him to help you better understand the things you read.

DAY 2
THE BIBLE WILL NEVER GO AWAY

Verse of the Day: Isaiah 40:8

Challenge: 1 Peter 1:25

 DO IT Circle the things that will last forever.

Did you circle the Bible? All of the other items will one day disappear.

How long is forever? How many years? Forever is FOREVER! (People have a hard time understanding forever.)

What about the Bible (not the "book" you own...but the words found in the Bible)? God's words will last forever.

 KNOW IT ☐ The teachings in the Bible will last forever (Isaiah 40:8).
☐ The Bible is given to us by God to teach, train, discipline, and grow us to look more like Jesus (2 Timothy 3:16-17).

 PRAY IT Thank God for the Bible. Praise Him for giving you His words that will last forever.

19

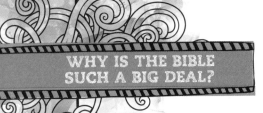
DAY 3
THE BIBLE IS A TRUE BOOK

Verse of the Day: Psalm 119:160

Challenge: John 8:31-32

 DO IT List three things you know are true. List three things you know are false.

TRUE	FALSE

Was the Bible on the "True" list?

 KNOW IT ☐ Many scientific truths are recorded as facts in the Bible such as the shape of the world as it hangs in space (Job 26:7-8; Isaiah 40:22).
☐ Ecclesiastes 1:7 tells how water from a stream returns to its source. Perhaps without even understanding it, the writer of Ecclesiastes recorded the process of the water cycle (evaporation, condensation, and precipitation) long before scientists figured it out.
☐ The stories in the Bible are *real* and *true* (John 17:17).

 PRAY IT Thank God for the Bible. Tell Him about your favorite Bible story. Thank Him for what the Bible teaches you.

DAY 4
THE BIBLE IS ALIVE

Verse of the Day: Hebrews 4:12

Challenge: Matthew 4:4

 DO IT How would you describe something that is alive? Draw pictures of six things in your house that are alive.

How do you know these things are alive? What do you think it means to say "the Bible is alive?"

 KNOW IT ☐ To say "the Bible is alive" means that the words continue to speak to people today. When you read the Bible, you learn how to honor God through the choices you make, the way you treat other people, and how you live. The Bible helps you know what to do (Hebrews 4:12).
☐ The Bible is for everyone—all peoples of the world. The Bible speaks to people in all languages and in every country of the world (Psalm 67:1-2).
☐ The Bible has been translated into hundreds of different languages. Some people still do not have the Bible in a language they can read and understand.

 PRAY IT Thank God for the Bible. Tell God one thing the Bible has taught you that you need to change. Ask for God's help in making this change.

 PARENT Talk It's time for a Parent Talk! Ask your mom and/or dad to tell you what their favorite Bible verse is and why. Be ready to tell them yours, too! Talk about what you are learning in the Bible and ask questions about things you don't understand.

DAY 5

THE BIBLE CHALLENGES PEOPLE TO RESPOND TO GOD

Verses of the Day: Proverbs 3:5-6

Challenge: 1 Peter 5:7

 DO IT Throughout Scripture, God challenges people to be and do certain things. Locate these three verses in your Bible. Read and match the verses to the correct statements.

ASK FOR WISDOM	ISAIAH 41:10
LOVE FOR ENEMIES	JAMES 1:5
DO NOT BE AFRAID	MATTHEW 5:44

Can you do these things this week? How? When? Where? Think of other things the Bible challenges you to do. Are you willing to do what God says?

 KNOW IT ☐ The Bible says that salvation through Jesus is a gift and that *everyone* by faith can receive God's gift (Ephesians 2:8-9).

☐ The Bible tells people how to obey God (Matthew 5-7).

☐ The Bible tells how people's lives were affected by their responses to God (Luke 18:18-23, John 4:39-42).

 PRAY IT Ask God to help you always respond in ways that please and honor Him.

DAY 6

THE BIBLE HELPS GUIDE PEOPLE'S LIVES

Verse of the Day: Psalm 119:105

Challenge: John 8:12

 DO IT Connect the dots to complete the picture. What is it? What purpose does a flashlight serve?

The Bible is like God's flashlight. It helps to guide or show us the way. What are some areas in your life where you need guidance?

Look at the following list. Do you need help with these areas? If the area where you need help is not listed, fill in the blanks.

☐ Obeying my parents

☐ Treating my brothers/sisters with respect

☐ Spending time completing my *Growing in my Faith* journal

☐ Telling my friends about God

☐ Sharing my toys

☐ _____

☐ _____

 KNOW IT ☐ The Bible helps me understand how God wants me to live (James 1:22-25).

☐ The Bible helps me make decisions (Proverbs 1:7).

☐ The Bible tells me how to love and serve God as well as how to treat other people (Exodus 20: 1-17).

 PRAY IT Ask God to help you trust and follow the teachings in the Bible.

THE BOOKS OF LAW

GENESIS (JEN ih siss) is about the beginning of things, including how God created the world and everything in it, the great flood, the Tower of Babel, and the beginnings of the nation of Israel.

LEVITICUS (lih VIT ih kuhs) continues the history told in the Book of Exodus. The book also contains the ceremonial and religious law.

EXODUS (EK suh duhs) tells about the people of Israel leaving (exodus) Egypt, how they wandered in the wilderness, and how God gave His law to the people of Israel.

DEUTERONOMY (doo tuh RAHN uh mee) contains a second telling of the giving of the Law. The book ends with Moses' death.

NUMBERS (NUHM buhrz) tells of the census or numbering of the people of Israel and the history of their journey after leaving Egypt.

THE OLD TESTAMENT CONSISTS OF 39 DIFFERENT BOOKS. THE BOOKS ARE SEPARATED INTO 5 DIVISIONS.

RUTH (ROOTH) contains the story of God's care for Naomi and her daughter-in-law, Ruth. The book also tells how Ruth met and married Boaz and had a son named Obed.

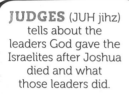

JUDGES (JUH jihz) tells about the leaders God gave the Israelites after Joshua died and what those leaders did.

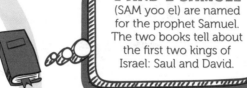

1 AND 2 SAMUEL (SAM yoo el) are named for the prophet Samuel. The two books tell about the first two kings of Israel: Saul and David.

1 AND 2 KINGS (KINGZ) continue the history of Israel from King Solomon through the division of Israel into two kingdoms, Israel and Judah, and into the exile of both kingdoms. These books cover a period of about 425 years.

JOSHUA (JAHSH yoo uh) tells how the Israelites entered and became the owners of the land God promised them.

1 AND 2 CHRONICLES (KRAHN ih kuhls) are the records of the history of Israel and Judah.

EZRA (EZ ruh) begins with the return from the exile. The book covers a period of about 80 years, telling of the rebuilding of the Jerusalem temple and how the Jews decided to obey God again.

OLD TESTAMENT HISTORY

NEHEMIAH (nee huh MIGH uh) continues the Jews' history with the return from exile and how God used Nehemiah to rebuild Jerusalem's city wall.

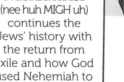

ESTHER (ESS tuhr) tells how Esther became queen and how she prevented the killing of the Jews.

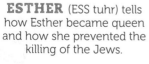

THE OLD TESTAMENT CONTAINS THE PROMISES OF GOD TO SEND JESUS!

POETRY

JOB (JOHB) is the story of a man named Job, whom God tested.

PSALMS (SAHLMZ) is a collection of one hundred fifty "songs" written by different authors over a long period of time. King David wrote many of the Psalms.

PROVERBS (PRAHV uhrbs) contains godly wisdom that helps people to live in ways that please God, gives practical advice, and makes wise observations.

ISAIAH (igh eye ZAY uh) includes prophecy about the coming of the Messiah.

ECCLESIASTES (ih klee zih ASST eez) is another book of wisdom written by Solomon.

MAJOR PROPHETS

JEREMIAH (jer ih MIGH uh) calls the people of Judah to turn away from their idol worship and other sins.

THE SONG OF SONGS (sahng-ahv sahngs) is a love poem that King Solomon wrote.

LAMENTATIONS (la men TAY shuhnz) is a lament, or a song of mourning, over the sins of Judah. Jeremiah wrote this book.

DANIEL (DAN yuhl) speaks of the power of God over people of all nations.

EZEKIEL (ih ZEE kih uhl) tells of God's judgment on Israel and other nations, but also predicts the future blessings of God and salvation of His people.

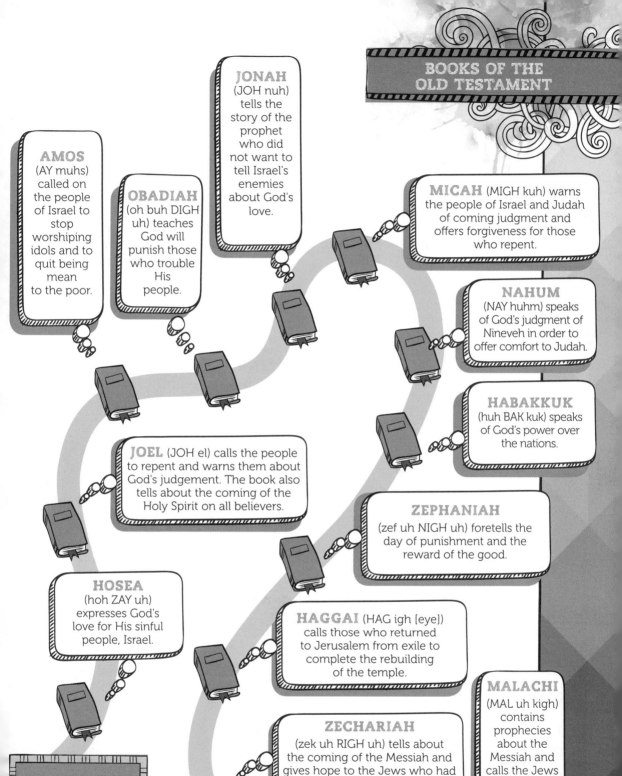

JONAH (JOH nuh) tells the story of the prophet who did not want to tell Israel's enemies about God's love.

AMOS (AY muhs) called on the people of Israel to stop worshiping idols and to quit being mean to the poor.

OBADIAH (oh buh DIGH uh) teaches God will punish those who trouble His people.

MICAH (MIGH kuh) warns the people of Israel and Judah of coming judgment and offers forgiveness for those who repent.

NAHUM (NAY huhm) speaks of God's judgment of Nineveh in order to offer comfort to Judah.

HABAKKUK (huh BAK kuk) speaks of God's power over the nations.

JOEL (JOH el) calls the people to repent and warns them about God's judgement. The book also tells about the coming of the Holy Spirit on all believers.

ZEPHANIAH (zef uh NIGH uh) foretells the day of punishment and the reward of the good.

HOSEA (hoh ZAY uh) expresses God's love for His sinful people, Israel.

HAGGAI (HAG igh [eye]) calls those who returned to Jerusalem from exile to complete the rebuilding of the temple.

MALACHI (MAL uh kigh) contains prophecies about the Messiah and calls the Jews in Jerusalem to turn from their sins and renew their relationship with God.

ZECHARIAH (zek uh RIGH uh) tells about the coming of the Messiah and gives hope to the Jews who had returned to Jerusalem from exile.

MINOR PROPHETS

25

HOW DO I STUDY THE BIBLE?

What's the point of reading the Bible? The point of reading the Bible goes back to God's plan for you. The Bible can help you become more like Jesus. But that doesn't really happen if you just look at the words and don't understand them or let them change you. We all need to learn to study the Bible so God uses it to change us.

This week we are going to look at different ways you can study your Bible. Whatever way you use to study the Bible, there are two things you should always do: ask questions and write down what you learn so you can remember. Look on pages 110-111 for more ideas on studying the Bible.

Here are some ways to study:

Study one Bible book. Begin with the first verse of a Bible book and read 10-12 verses a day. Think about these questions as you read the verses:

- What is the book about?
- What do these verses say about God?
- What is God saying to the people?
- What am I supposed to do?

You could also study your Bible by studying one Bible verse. Certain words or concepts like love, forgiveness, or joy are found throughout the Bible. Choose a word and find a verse or verses in the Bible that contain that word. Read the verses before and after the verse to help you understand it. Think about these questions when you study a word or concept:

- What can I learn from the verse?
- What does it teach me about God?
- What are the important words?
- What am I supposed to do?

Another way to study the Bible is to learn about people in the Bible. What do you know about Esther or David or Paul? Their stories are in the Bible for a reason—to help us learn and become more like Jesus. Think about these questions when you study a Bible person:

- What took place in this person's life?
- How does this person teach me about God?
- What can I learn from the person?
- What am I supposed to do?

Just like most things, studying the Bible takes practice. The more you do it, the easier it gets and the better you will be at it. Always remember: the Bible is a living book that will help you become more like Jesus. Look for the changes you need to make in your life.

"Help me understand your instruction and I will obey it and follow it with all my heart." Psalm 119:34

STUDY ONE BIBLE BOOK:
A VERSE-BY-VERSE STUDY OF THE BOOK OF MARK PART 1

Verses of the Day: Mark 1:1-8

Challenge: Isaiah 40:3

 DO IT Imagine God told you to write a book about Jesus.

What would you write in your book? What would you name the book? Draw a picture of the cover of your book.

Read Mark 1:1-8. Then answer these questions.

What is God saying to the people in these verses?

What are the important words in these verses?

What do these verses mean I am supposed to do?

 KNOW IT ☐ The Book of Mark was written by a Jewish man named Mark.

☐ Mark wrote about Jesus as the ultimate servant.

☐ Mark wrote a book full of action, showing Jesus always on the go.

☐ Mark uses the word *immediately* over 40 times in his book.

 PRAY IT Ask God to help you learn more about Jesus as you study the Book of Mark. Ask Him to help you plan and prepare for your time with Him.

DAY 2

STUDY ONE BIBLE BOOK:
A VERSE-BY-VERSE STUDY OF THE BOOK OF MARK PART 2

Verses of the Day: Mark 1:9-13

Challenge: Matthew 3:13–4:1

 DO IT How would you answer these questions about Mark 1:9-13?

What is God saying to the people in these verses?

What do these verses teach me about God and Jesus?

What do these verses mean I am supposed to do?

 DO IT Draw a picture of what you think Jesus' baptism looked like. Draw a picture of your baptism. What is the same in the pictures? What is different?

JESUS' BAPTISM

MY BAPTISM

 KNOW IT ☐ Baptism is a public declaration of faith in Jesus and being put under water and brought back up to tell others in the church that you have become a Christian (Romans 6:3-4).

☐ Jesus was baptized even though He never sinned. When a person is baptized, she is following Jesus' example (Matthew 3:14-15).

☐ A *wilderness* is an area of land with little rainfall and few people, more like what we would call a *desert*.

☐ To *tempt* someone is to try to get a person to make a wrong choice or take action that is wrong.

 PRAY IT Tell God things you are sometimes tempted to do. Ask God to help you not give in to the temptations.

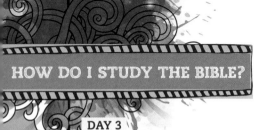

DAY 3
STUDY ONE BIBLE VERSE

Verse of the Day: Ephesians 6:1

Challenge: Exodus 20:1-17

 Circle the people and things you obey.

Why do you obey these people and things?

What would happen if you did not obey them?

 Read Ephesians 6:1 together in 3-4 different translations. Use a Bible app to search translations. Discuss any different words used in the translations.

Write Ephesians 6:1 in your own words:

What does this verse teach me about God?

What am I supposed to do?

 ☐ Obey means "to hear God's Word and act on it."
☐ When a person hears or reads God's Word, he needs to obey what he hears or reads. To really hear God's Word means to obey God's Word (James 1:22).
☐ The word *obey* or a form of it is in the Bible 140 times! Read 1 Samuel 15:22 and Acts 5:29. What do these verses say to do?

 Ask God to help you obey Him every day.

DAY 4
STUDY PEOPLE IN THE BIBLE: BABIES OF THE BIBLE

Verse of the Day: Luke 2:12

Challenge: Luke 2:4-14

 Draw things you can think of that babies need.

Read these Bible verses. Beside each one, write the name of the baby the verses tell about.

Exodus 2:1-10

Luke 1:57-60

Luke 2:4-7

 ☐ The Bible shows us babies are important to God (Exodus 2:1-10).
☐ The Bible shows us God has plans for babies even before they are born (Psalm 139:13).
☐ The Bible shows us God helps parents take care of babies (2 Timothy 1:5).

 Thank God for caring for you when you were a baby.

DAY 5

STUDY PEOPLE IN THE BIBLE:
JOHN THE BAPTIST PART 1

Verses of the Day: Matthew 3:1-6

Challenge: Luke 1:57-60

 DO IT When you hear the name "John the Baptist" what comes to mind? Answer these questions about John.

Draw a picture of John the Baptist.

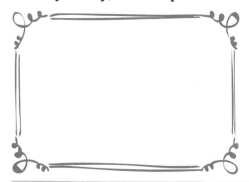

What did John teach? (Matthew 3:2-3)

What did John wear and eat? (Matthew 3:4)

How did people respond to John? (Matthew 3:5-6)

 KNOW IT ☐ John the Baptist was related to Jesus (Luke 1:18-25, 36, 39-45; 57-80).
☐ John's father, Zechariah, was a priest. (Luke 1:5).
☐ Because Zechariah did not believe he would have a son, he was unable to speak until after John's birth (Luke 1:8-20, 57-80).
☐ John's birth was announced by the angel Gabriel (Luke 1:11-20).

PRAY IT Ask God to give you the courage to tell people about Jesus too.

DAY 6

STUDY PEOPLE IN THE BIBLE:
JOHN THE BAPTIST, PART 2

Verses of the Day: Matthew 3:13-17

Challenge: Luke 1:11-20

 DO IT Think about the things you learned about John the Baptist in yesterday's study. Answer these questions about John.

When and where did John the Baptist live? (Matthew 3:1)

What did John do in today's Bible study? (Matthew 3:15)

What does John the Baptist teach me about God?

 KNOW IT ☐ John the Baptist believed Jesus is God's Son (John 1:29).
☐ John told people things they did that did not please God (Matthew 3:7).
☐ John obeyed Jesus and baptized Him even when he did not understand (Matthew 3:14-15).

 PRAY IT God teaches us to boldly tell others about Jesus. Pray and ask God to give you boldness to tell others about His love for them.

BOOKS OF THE NEW TESTAMENT

GOSPELS

MATTHEW (MATH yoo) was originally written for the Jews and shows Jesus as the Messiah and King.

MARK (MAHRK) was written for the Gentiles (non-Jews), and presents Jesus as the Son of Man.

ACTS (AKTS) tells what the apostles did during the time after Jesus' crucifixion, resurrection, and return to heaven. Luke wrote this book and reported the coming of the Holy Spirit and the growth of the church.

JOHN (JAHN) emphasizes Jesus is the Son of God and that by believing in Him, people can have eternal life.

LUKE (LEWK) was written to the Greeks. Luke wrote about Jesus' humanity and His death on the cross.

NEW TESTAMENT HISTORY

PAUL'S LETTERS

1 AND 2 CORINTHIANS (koh RIN thih uhns) were letters written to the Christians at Corinth in Greece. Paul wrote about sin in the church at Corinth and stressed church unity. Paul defended his own authority and spoke against the false teachers in Corinth.

GALATIANS (guh LAY shuhnz) was written to the Christians in the province of Galatia, in Asia Minor. The theme is the freedom of the gospel as opposed to the bondage of the law.

PHILIPPIANS (fih LIP ih uhnz) was written to the church in Philippi. Paul thanked the believers for their kindness towards him and explained true joy in Christ.

ROMANS (ROH muhnz) was written to Christians in Rome and is about living in ways that please God because of faith in Him.

EPHESIANS (ih FEE shuhnz) was written to teach Christians they have been saved by grace and should live like God wants them to live so that they can stand against the ways of Satan.

COLOSSIANS (kuh LAHSH uhnz) encouraged the church in Colossae to obey Jesus' teachings and warned the people to stay away from teachings that are not true.

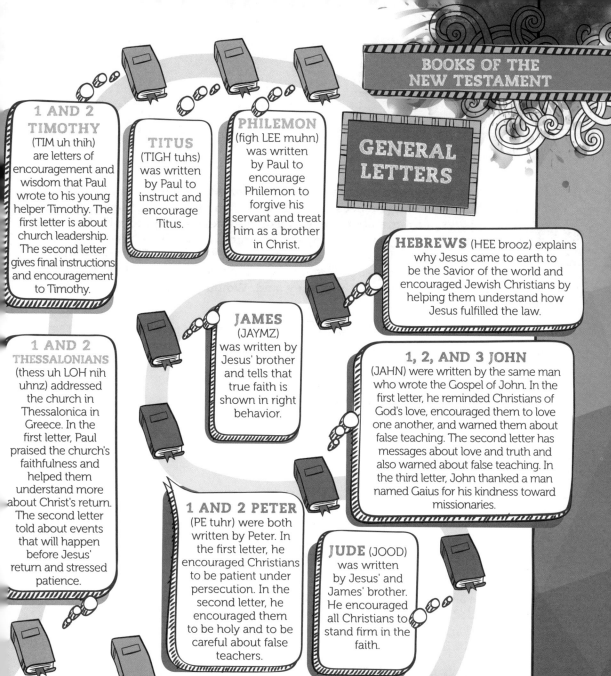

1 AND 2 TIMOTHY
(TIM uh thih) are letters of encouragement and wisdom that Paul wrote to his young helper Timothy. The first letter is about church leadership. The second letter gives final instructions and encouragement to Timothy.

TITUS
(TIGH tuhs) was written by Paul to instruct and encourage Titus.

PHILEMON
(figh LEE muhn) was written by Paul to encourage Philemon to forgive his servant and treat him as a brother in Christ.

GENERAL LETTERS

HEBREWS
(HEE brooz) explains why Jesus came to earth to be the Savior of the world and encouraged Jewish Christians by helping them understand how Jesus fulfilled the law.

1 AND 2 THESSALONIANS
(thess uh LOH nih uhnz) addressed the church in Thessalonica in Greece. In the first letter, Paul praised the church's faithfulness and helped them understand more about Christ's return. The second letter told about events that will happen before Jesus' return and stressed patience.

JAMES
(JAYMZ) was written by Jesus' brother and tells that true faith is shown in right behavior.

1, 2, AND 3 JOHN
(JAHN) were written by the same man who wrote the Gospel of John. In the first letter, he reminded Christians of God's love, encouraged them to love one another, and warned them about false teaching. The second letter has messages about love and truth and also warned about false teaching. In the third letter, John thanked a man named Gaius for his kindness toward missionaries.

1 AND 2 PETER
(PE tuhr) were both written by Peter. In the first letter, he encouraged Christians to be patient under persecution. In the second letter, he encouraged them to be holy and to be careful about false teachers.

JUDE
(JOOD) was written by Jesus' and James' brother. He encouraged all Christians to stand firm in the faith.

REVELATION
(rev uh LAY shuhn) was written by John. He encouraged and warned Christians about events leading to the end of time and the coming of "a new heaven and a new earth."

NEW TESTAMENT PROPHESY

THE NEW TESTAMENT HAS 27 DIFFERENT BOOKS.
THE BOOKS ARE SEPARATED INTO 5 DIVISIONS.

WHAT ABOUT PRAYER?

Think of a time when you met someone new. At first you didn't know them at all, but over time you became friends. Are you thinking of someone like that? Now try to remember *how* you became friends. You probably became friends by learning you had things in common. Maybe you liked to do the same things or you laughed at the same kinds of things. Now try to imagine what would have happened if you met that person but you never talked to them or listened to anything they said. Would you have become friends? No, of course not!

Talking with and listening to another person is the way we get to know them. That is exactly how it is with God. Now that you have a personal relationship with Him, He wants you to communicate with Him. He knows all about you and He wants you to know about Him. You talk to God and listen to Him through prayer.

Sometimes we think prayer is too hard and we are afraid we won't get it right. It helps to remember how much God loves you and that He *wants* you to talk to Him. Even Jesus' disciples weren't sure they could get it right. They asked Jesus, "Lord, teach us to pray." Then Jesus gave them an example to follow, a model prayer. We will be looking at it this week.

You can pray to God anywhere and at any time. You can stand up, sit down, lie down, or run around when you pray. You can pray with your eyes opened or closed. Sometimes closing our eyes helps us to focus on God, but you definitely can pray with your eyes open, especially if you pray while you ride your bike! Prayer is one of the very best ways we have to get to know God. Prayer is personal. It is just between you and God.

Prayer is also powerful! The Bible tells many stories of how God hears and answers prayer. God's answers to prayers have freed people from prison, closed the mouths of hungry lions, and caused fire to rain down from heaven. The Bible promises when you pray, God will hear and answer your prayers—but in His own way.

Prayer is NOT just a way to get what we want. It is a way to talk to God about what we want and then to trust Him to take care of what we ask. He knows much better than we do what is best for us. Often you will see God give you something better than you could have imagined. When you see that, you are learning more about who God is and how much He loves you. That's really what prayer is all about!

"Rejoice always; pray constantly; give thanks in everything; for this is God's will for you in Christ Jesus." I Thessalonians 5:17

DAY 1
WHAT IS PRAYER?

Verse of the Day: Psalm 17:6

Challenge: Daniel 6:13-22

 DO IT What is prayer? Fill in the blanks below.

Prayer is T _____ to and
L _____ to God.

It's simple! God wants us to talk to Him. He wants us to listen to Him. To remind yourself, try this. Write this message on several sticky notes. Place the notes in places you will see every day.

Dear _____,
I'd really like to talk with you today.
Love, God

Some people like to write prayers down. Does God hear those prayers? Of course He does! He knows our thoughts, and when we direct our thoughts to Him through what we write, He hears us. Try it now. Write down what you would like to say to God.

 KNOW IT
☐ Prayer means talking and listening to God.
☐ God wants you to share concerns with Him (1 Peter 5:7).
☐ God hears your prayers 24/7 (24 hours a day, 7 days a week).
☐ God will answer your prayer (1 John 5:14-15).

 PRAY IT Thank God, the Creator of the universe, for inviting you to talk with Him.

DAY 2
MODEL PRAYER

Verses of the Day: Matthew 6:9-13

Challenge: Luke 11:1-4

 DO IT **If you could ask Jesus to explain anything, what is something you would ask Him? Write your question here.**

The disciples could ask Jesus anything, and they asked Him, "Lord, how do we pray?"

Jesus didn't just tell them. He showed them by giving an example. Sometimes we call it the Lord's Prayer. You may already know it. It is printed below. Read this prayer in Matthew 6:9-13. Use the word search to find the missing words.

"Our _____ in heaven, your name be honored as holy. Your _____ come, your will be done on earth as it is in _____. Give us today our daily _____; And forgive us our debts as we also have forgiven our debtors. And do not bring us into temptation but _____ us from the evil one."

```
K I N G D O M
I B D S J N Y
N R L K O H F
H E A V E N B
F A T H E R R
K D F A T H E
D E L I V E R
```

 KNOW IT
☐ Jesus, God's Son, taught His disciples how to pray (Matthew 6:9-13).
☐ You can follow the examples, commands, and teachings of Jesus (Psalm 32:8).
☐ God is everywhere at all times. He hears everything you say to Him (Psalm 139:7-10).

PRAY IT Thank God for sending Jesus to teach you how to pray.

DAY 3
HOW DO I PRAY

Verse of the Day: Ephesians 6:18

Challenge: Daniel 6:10-23

 DO IT Read the words on each finger and write the first letter of that word below. (If the "Y" doesn't make sense to you yet, that's OK. It will in a minute.)

⬤ stands for PRAISE. *Praise God for all He has done for you.*

⬤ stands for REPENT. *Repent means "to turn away or change from disobeying God to obeying Him."*

⬤ stands for ASK. *God wants you to ask Him for the things you and other people need.*

⬤ stands for YOURSELF. *God wants you to pray for yourself. Tell Him what you need or even want. He loves you.*

 KNOW IT ☐ In the Lord's Prayer, Jesus showed that it is good to begin our prayers with praise to God (Matthew 6:9-11).
☐ The Bible tells us that when we sin, if we repent we will be forgiven (1 John 1:9). God wants us to pray for other people (James 5:16).
☐ God wants us to share our cares and concerns with Him (Philippians 4:6).

 PRAY IT Using your hand as a guide, praise God, repent of your sin, and ask Him for things for others and yourself.

 PARENT Talk Using your own hand, show your parent what you learned today about how to pray. Spend time praying together.

DAY 4
PRAYER IS POWERFUL

Verse of the Day: James 5:16

Challenge: Daniel 3:16-25

 DO IT If you could design your own superhero, what would this person look like? Draw your hero in the space below. What would make your hero different from a regular person? What special powers would your hero have?

Would you like to have the same powers as your superhero? What would you do with your powers?

A superhero's powers are imaginary (made up—not real), but the power of prayer is REAL. The Bible says God hears and answers our prayers (1 John 5:14-15).

 KNOW IT ☐ The Bible is full of true stories about the power of prayer (1 Kings 18:16-39, Acts 12:5-11).
☐ Paul and Silas prayed and were freed from prison (Acts 16:25-34).
☐ Samson prayed for his strength to return (Judges 16:28).
☐ Elijah prayed for a dead boy to be brought back to life and the boy was revived (1 Kings 17:17-23).

 PRAY IT Thank God for being able to pray to Him. Ask Him to meet your needs and the needs of others according to His will.

DAY 5
PRAYER IS PERSONAL

Verses of the Day: Philippians 4:6-7

Challenge: 1 Samuel 1:10-17

STOP! Right where you are, be as still as you can be. Now close your eyes and focus on God.

THINK! Think about the things that worry you. What do you think about when you go to bed at night? What hurts you and you wish could be different? What makes you sad? Your family? School? Friends?

PRAY! Now, whatever you are thinking of—those things that make you sad or worried—tell God. Just say, "God, I am sad about_____. I am worried about _____." You *can* say it out loud, but you don't have to. God hears you.

God's Word says to pray always and to give your cares to Him. He'll take care of them. He loves you!

 DO IT Hold this book in front of a mirror to discover four important things about prayer.

GOD WILL HEAR YOU WHEN PRAY

GOD ANSWERS PRAYER WITH YES, NO, OR WAIT.

GOD KNOWS WHAT IS BEST FOR YOU.

 KNOW IT ☐ God is all-powerful. He can handle all your cares and concerns.
☐ God is all-knowing. He knows what you need and want, but He wants you to tell Him about your worries.
☐ Nothing is too big or small to tell God. God loves you and wants to develop a close relationship with you through prayer.

 PRAY IT Ask God to help you stop worrying and trust Him more each day.

DAY 6
PRAYING FOR OTHERS

Verse of the Day: Ephesians 6:18

Challenge: Ephesians 6:16-20

 DO IT Look at the faces of these people. Do any of them remind you of someone you know? If they do, write the names of the people you know on or near the faces of people like them. Now think about the names you have written. What do you know about these people? What do you think they need? How can you pray for them?

Part of growing as a Christian means praying for others. We need to be aware of the people around us and how we can pray for them.

 KNOW IT ☐ The Bible is full of examples of people praying for others:
☐ Moses prayed for the Israelites and God did not punish them (Exodus 32:11-14).
☐ Jesus prayed for His followers (John 17:20).
☐ The church prayed for Peter and he was freed from prison (Acts 12:5-11).
☐ Elijah prayed for Israel and God sent fire from heaven (1 Kings 18:36-39).
☐ God always hears and answers prayers.

 PRAY IT Ask God to bless the people whose names you wrote above. Ask God to make you more aware of the people around you each day.

35

A prayer journal is a book where you write down information about your prayer requests. Writing down your prayer requests allows you to see how God has worked and is continuing to work in your life. Check out this page of a prayer journal.

DATE	MY PRAYER REQUEST	HOW GOD ANSWERED	DATE GOD ANSWERED
Monday 3/2	I need help learning to spell the words for my spelling test.		
Tuesday 3/3	Marcia is going to visit her aunt and uncle this weekend.		
Tuesday 3/4	My grandpa's shoulder surgery is tomorrow.	Grandpa did not have any problems with his surgery.	3/5
Wednesday 3/5	Grandpa's shoulder surgery	Grandpa is feeling much better. He should get to go home Saturday.	3/6
Wednesday 3/5	Spelling test tomorrow		

Notice the boxes under "How God Answered" and "Date God Answered" are not filled in for three of the requests. These events have not taken place yet. After the test, these boxes can be filled in to show how God answered the prayer.

When Marcia returns, information can be written about her trip.

HERE ARE SOME THINGS YOU CAN DO TO KEEP A PRAYER JOURNAL.

- Ask your parents to buy you a notebook.

- Draw and label columns like the ones below.

- Write or draw pictures to represent your prayer requests. (It's OK to have more than one request each day.)

- Write or draw how God answered your prayers (after He does so).

- Fill in the date God answered your prayers.

- Look back at the ways God answered your prayers.

- Keep your prayer journal in a special place. (It is OK to keep your prayer requests private.)

REMEMBER

God answers prayers in three ways:

 YES. He will give you what you asked for.

 NO. He will not give you what you asked for.

 WAIT. You will have to wait for Him to answer you.

DATE	MY PRAYER REQUEST	HOW GOD ANSWERED	DATE GOD ANSWERED

God knows what is best for us!

HOW DO I HEAR GOD SPEAK TO ME?

Do you have a close friend or family member you haven't seen in a while? Think about that person. If you could choose to get a text from them or to a video call, which one would you choose? Texts are great, but hearing a friend's voice is probably better. If your friend or family member called you, would you recognize their voice? You probably would if you have a close relationship with them.

The Bible teaches us that God speaks to us. He wants us to recognize His voice. Do you want to hear God? How do you know when God is speaking to you? It can be difficult to know because we don't usually "hear" God's voice out loud. It is natural to wonder whether what you are "hearing" is from God or just your own thoughts.

If you think God is speaking to you, but you wonder whether it is really God, here are some questions to think about.

- *Is the message I hear in agreement with the Bible?* God will never tell you anything that goes against the Bible.
- *Is the message I am hearing true?* God will never say anything that's not true.
- *Does the message I am hearing line up with who God is?* God will never tell you anything that goes against who He is.

God speaks to people in different ways. These are some ways God speaks to us.

→ God speaks to us through His Word, the Bible.
→ God speaks to us through prayer. Remember that prayer is talking to and *listening* to God.
→ God speaks to us through situations in our lives.
→ God speaks to us through other people.
→ God speaks to us through the Holy Spirit.

Learning to listen to God takes practice. It is probably easy to recognize your parents' voices because you are so used to hearing them. You will get used to hearing God's voice, too. The longer you listen, the easier it will be to recognize His voice.

You may feel that it is difficult to hear God speak to you. Many things can keep you from listening to God. Your sins, thoughts, desires, dreams, as well as other people can keep you from hearing God. If you are not sure what you hear is from God, ask Him to continue talking with you and to help you know for sure what you hear is from Him. This week's Bible studies will help you learn to listen to God more.

"My sheep hear my voice. I know them and they follow me." John 10:27

DAY 1
GOD SPEAKS THROUGH THE BIBLE

Verses of the Day: 2 Timothy 3:15-16

Challenge: Psalm 119:11

DO IT You already know some things God has told you. Answer the questions below:

Should I ☐ tell a lie or ☐ tell the truth?

Should I ☐ obey my parents or ☐ do what I want?

How does God feel about me?

Should I ☐ put myself first, or should I ☐ first think about God and others?

How did you know the answers to these questions?

KNOW IT ☐ One of the major ways God speaks to us is through His Word, the Bible.

☐ Studying the Bible helps you know what God wants you to do.

☐ In the Bible, God clearly tells you what you should do in many different situations.

☐ You don't have to wonder about the right thing when it is written in the Bible.

☐ What God says in the Bible will never change.

☐ Every word and every story in the Bible is there for a reason. When you read a Bible verse or story, listen to what God is saying to you.

PRAY IT Thank God for the Bible. Ask Him to help you hear Him speak as you read and study your Bible.

DAY 2
GOD SPEAKS THROUGH PRAYER

Verse of the Day: 1 Thessalonians 5:17

Challenge: Hebrews 3:15

DO IT Look at the drawings below. Be still and say (out loud or silently) the suggested sentences to God. Then practice listening by just being still. Write in the second empty bubble what you think God is saying back to you.

YOU TO GOD: I love you.   GOD TO YOU:

YOU TO GOD: How can I show love to my family today?   GOD TO YOU:

YOU TO GOD: I am sorry.   GOD TO YOU:

This is a way to begin practicing listening to God in prayer. You will find that the more you practice, the easier it is to hear Him.

KNOW IT ☐ God hears every time you pray.

☐ God speaks to you and will answer your prayers.

☐ God wants you to learn to know His voice.

PRAY IT Ask God to help you hear and understand His voice when He speaks to you. Ask, "God, do you have something to say to me?" Then be still and listen for several minutes.

DAY 3
GOD SPEAKS THROUGH SITUATIONS AND EVENTS

Verses of the Day: Genesis 50:19-21

Challenge: Proverbs 21:1

 DO IT Write down some things you will do today. How would you know if God spoke to you during one of these events or activities? How would you feel? How would you recognize God's voice?

When God speaks to us through situations, it usually happens in a way that He is directing us to do a specific thing. Here's an example: A new kid comes to your class in school. You keep thinking that you should be his friend. Over and over the thought comes to you that you should talk to the new person. That might be God talking to you.

 KNOW IT
☐ God can speak to you any way He desires.
☐ God spoke to Noah and told Him to build the ark (Genesis 6:13-22).
☐ God spoke to Moses through a burning bush (Exodus 3).
☐ God spoke to Daniel and his friends when they were captives (Daniel 1:3-21).

 PRAY IT God knows about every situation in your life, and He wants to help you. Ask Him to help you know how to handle the situations. Ask, "God, do you have something to say to me?" Then be still and listen for several minutes.

 PARENT Talk Time for a Parent Talk! Ask your parents to tell you a time they heard God speak to them or answer one of their prayers.

DAY 4
GOD SPEAKS THROUGH PEOPLE

Verse of the Day: Joshua 3:9

Challenge: Joshua 3:9-17

 DO IT Draw a face to resemble someone you listen to. What are some things this person says to you? Does what this person say about God help you know more about Him?

 KNOW IT ☐ In the Bible, God spoke to people through prophets, priests, and people such as Peter, John, and Paul. Who was the most important person God spoke through in the Bible? Jesus! (Hebrews 1:1-2)
☐ God speaks through people today. He speaks through your pastor, teachers, parents, and other people. These people must be careful to make sure what they say matches what God says in the Bible.

 PRAY IT Pray for the people who speak to you about God. Ask God to help the people clearly understand and communicate what God says to them. Ask, "God, do you have something to say to me?" Then be still and listen for several minutes.

DAY 5
GOD SPEAKS THROUGH THE HOLY SPIRIT

Verse of the Day: John 16:13

Challenge: Romans 8:26

DO IT Use the code below to decode the statement.

_ _ _   _ _ _ _ _   _ _ _ _ _ _
20 8 5   8 15 12 25   19 16 9 18 9 20

_ _ _ _ _   _ _ _ _ _ _ _ _ _   _ _ _ _ ,
8 5 12 16 19   2 5 12 9 5 22 5 18 19   11 14 15 23

_ _ _ _ _ _ _ _ _ _ _ _ _ ,   _ _ _
21 14 4 5 18 19 20 1 14 4   1 14 4

_ _ _ _ _ _ _ _ _   _ _ _ _ _   _ _ _ _ _ _ _
18 5 13 5 13 2 5 18   1 12 12   20 8 9 14 7 19

_ _ _ _ _ _ .
1 2 15 21 20   7 15 4

KNOW IT
☐ The Holy Spirit is a special helper sent by God to help Christians know how to live.
☐ The Holy Spirit helps believers grow in their relationships with God and people.
☐ The Holy Spirit helps people recognize when God is speaking to them.

PRAY IT Thank God for the Holy Spirit. Ask God to help you listen to and understand what the Holy Spirit says. Ask, "God, do you have something to say to me?" Then be still and listen for several minutes.

DAY 6
GOD SPEAKS THROUGH YOUR THOUGHTS

Verses of the Day: Romans 12:1-2

Challenge: Psalm 139:2

DO IT Because God often speaks to us by directing our thoughts, it can be difficult to know which thoughts come from our own brains and which thoughts are God speaking to us. Look at the thoughts below and put a star by the ones you think are probably ideas that God directed.

I AM SORRY I WAS MEAN TO MY BROTHER.

I SHOULD CLEAN MY ROOM LIKE MY MOTHER SAID.

I WANT SOME ICE CREAM.

MY SISTER NEEDS ME TO SAY ENCOURAGING WORDS TO HER.

I DON'T WANT TO GO TO CHURCH SUNDAY.

I COULD PRETEND TO BE SICK AND STAY HOME FROM SCHOOL.

KNOW IT
☐ God knows everything you think (even before you think it).
☐ God wants you to think about things pleasing to Him that will help you.
☐ God speaks to you through your thoughts.
☐ When you feel guilty for thinking something, that may be the Holy Spirit telling you to stop thinking about it.

PRAY IT Ask God to help you have thoughts that are positive and pleasing to Him. Ask Him to help you recognize when He is speaking to you through your thoughts. Ask, "God, do you have something to say to me?" Then be still and listen for several minutes.

MEMORIZING? HELP!

Since the Bible is one of the main ways God speaks to us, it is good to memorize Bible verses so we can have them with us all the time. This is part of what it means to "hide God's Word in your heart" (Psalm 119:11). To practice memorizing, you have a weekly memory verse in each section of this journal. Can you learn one verse a week? YES! You can!

On these two pages you will find some ideas that might help you. For practice, you could use this week's verse: "My *sheep hear my voice. I know them and they follow me*" John 10:27.

WRITE IT OUT

Writing the verse helps you look at one word at a time. Don't forget the Scripture reference. Learn that too!

VISUALIZE IT

Put the verse where you will see it many times. Write it more than once! Use sticky notes and put them on your mirror and in other places around the house. If your parents say it's OK, write the verse on your mirror with a dry erase marker. After you learn it, just wipe it off.

BREAK IT UP

This is an easy verse to break up! First, learn *My sheep hear my voice.* Then add *I know them.* Next add *and they follow me.* And finally learn John 10:27.

MAKE A GAME

Write each word on small slips of paper. Mix up the pieces of paper, then put the words in order again.

SING IT

Put the words of a verse to the tune of a song you know really well and sing it to yourself or someone in your family. Try *Row, Row, Row Your Boat* or *Twinkle, Twinkle Little Star.*

PICTURE IT

Sometimes you can picture the parts of a verse in your mind. Imagine a sheep with a really big ear, hearing a voice. Then a shepherd waving to the sheep and the sheep following him. Picture that!

USE HAND MOTIONS

Make up your own hand motions to help you learn a verse. *My sheep hear my voice:* A hand cupped at an ear. *I know them:* An index finger pointed to the side of the head (indicating knowing). *And they follow me:* Two fingers "walking."

RECORD IT

Do you have a way to record yourself reading the verse? If you do, ask your parents if you can read and record the verse. Then listen to it over and over until you can say it from memory.

MAKE IT UP

Make up your own tricks! Use rhymes to help you remember the main words (HEAR, KNOW, FOLLOW could be CHEER, GLOW, SWALLOW) or you could make up a sentence with the first letters of the verse or phrase.

KEEP IT UP

Once you memorize verses, remember what you've learned. Keep the papers with the verses on them in a special place. If your parents say it's OK, you might mark memorized verses in your Bible. You want to remember them forever!

LEARN IT TOGETHER

It's always more fun to learn together. You can make it a Family Challenge. Who can learn the fastest? You can say it together in different ways—with your tongue stuck out, in a whisper voice, or holding your nose.

WHO IS GOD?

Most people who think about God have questions about Him. Do you have questions too? Maybe some of your questions are like these:

- What does God look like?
- Where does God live?
- Who made God?
- What is God doing right now?

Those are all good questions. Some of your questions about God may have answers that are just too big for anyone to understand. This week we will learn about some things we can know about God.

The Bible tells us some things about God we can know for sure.

- **God is the one and only true God.** Some people believe in more than one god, but there is only one true God. He is God the Father, God the Son, and God the Holy Spirit (the Trinity). He has always existed. No one created God. He always has been and always will be. God will live forever.

- **God wants you to know who He is.** The Bible says to seek God. When you seek something, you look for it. God is everywhere. God sees, hears, and knows everything you do. God promised He will never leave you or turn away from you.

- **God wants to have a relationship with you.** God sent His Son Jesus to make a way for your sins to be forgiven so you can have a relationship with God. God *wants* to forgive you. He wants you to pray and spend time talking and listening to Him.

- **God can do anything and everything.** No one or no thing can limit God's powers. He has more power than the weather. He controls the sun, moon, and stars. He is in control of everything. God is all-powerful.

- **God is in control.** Although it may not always seem like it, God is in control of what happens in our world. He allows people to make choices which can cause bad things to happen, but God is always working for our ultimate good.

It is exciting to know that the God who created the universe wants to have a relationship with you! Learning more about God will always help us become more like Jesus.

"Know that the Lord your God is God." Deuteronomy 7:9a

PARENT Talk Parents, this week's memory verse is a good one for the whole family to memorize together. Take the time to learn this with your child and repeat it to each other frequently. Let this become a way your family encourages one another to trust God this week.

DAY 1
GOD IS CREATOR

Verse of the Day: Genesis 1:1

Challenge: Genesis 1:31–2:3

DO IT

THINK! What is the difference in these two words? CREATOR and CREATED?

Look at these pictures. Put a circle around all the items that are *created* and a square around all the items that are *Creator*.

KNOW IT

☐ God was not created. He has always been and always will be.

☐ Our God is the only Creator. Only God can make something from nothing.

☐ God created the world in six days and rested on the seventh day.

☐ God created a beautiful world for you to enjoy.

☐ God is the Creator of every person in the world.

PRAY IT

Thank God for the world He created. Thank Him for creating you and your family. Praise Him for being the awesome Creator. (You can say words like this: "God, I praise you because you are an amazing Creator God.")

DAY 2
GOD IS ALL—POWERFUL

Verse of the Day: Deuteronomy 3:24

Challenge: 1 Kings 18:36-38

DO IT

What makes something powerful? Rate these things from most powerful (1) to least powerful (4).

Think about the power of each item. Compare each item to God's power. Which is more powerful, God or the item?

How powerful is God? (Place an X on the line below to show how powerful you think God is.)

NOT POWERFUL ——————————— VERY POWERFUL

KNOW IT

Here are just a few things God can do:

☐ Heal (Psalm 30:2)

☐ Protect (Daniel 6:20-21)

☐ Provide (Philippians 4:19)

☐ Answer prayer (Psalm 17:6)

☐ Raise Jesus from the dead (Acts 4:10)

☐ ALL things (Mark 10:27)

PRAY IT

Praise God for His amazing power. ("God, I praise You because You are all-powerful.")

DAY 3
GOD KNOWS ALL

Verse of the Day: Psalm 147:5

Challenge: Psalm 139:1-6

DO IT

Test your brain:

Do you know the answers to these questions? God does. He knows everything!

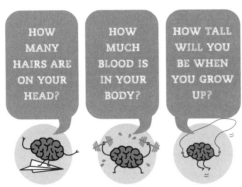

| HOW MANY HAIRS ARE ON YOUR HEAD? | HOW MUCH BLOOD IS IN YOUR BODY? | HOW TALL WILL YOU BE WHEN YOU GROW UP? |

Think about these things:

How do you feel knowing God knows all about you?

Is there anything you wish God did not know about you?

Is there anything you need to ask God to forgive you for thinking, saying, or doing?

KNOW IT

☐ God knows everything you think, say, and do.
☐ God knows everywhere you go.
☐ God knows everything you need.
☐ God knows what will happen in your future.

PRAY IT

Thank God that He knows all things about you. Ask Him to forgive you of things you think, say, and do that do not please Him. Praise God for being the all-knowing God.

DAY 4
GOD IS THE ONE TRUE GOD

Verse of the Day: Isaiah 46:9

Challenge: Isaiah 44:6, 8

DO IT

Test your brain:

How many stars can you count at night?

How many cars do you see every day?

How many friends do you have?

How many people live in your city?

Are all these numbers more than one? How many things can you list that there is only one of?

KNOW IT

☐ The Bible says there is only ONE true God (Isaiah 46:9).
☐ God does not want you to worship other gods (Exodus 20:4).
☐ God wants you to use His name only in ways that show respect for Him (Exodus 20:7).
☐ God wants you to love Him with all that you are. (Deuteronomy 6:5).

PRAY IT

Praise God for being the one true God. Ask Him to help you keep Him most important in your life.

DAY 5
GOD IS IN CONTROL

Verse of the Day: Psalm 115:3

Challenge: Psalm 93:1

DO IT Each item on the left controls something on the Right. Match the pairs!

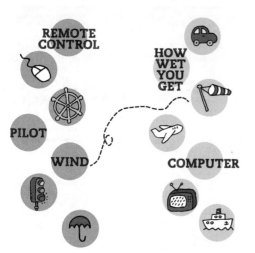

REMOTE CONTROL

HOW WET YOU GET

PILOT

WIND

COMPUTER

These people or things do have some control, but it is limited. Now think of God who can control everything!

KNOW IT
☐ God is in control of *everything.*
☐ God controls the weather, the stars, the wind, and the rain.
☐ Even when we don't see it and it may not feel like it, God is still in control.
☐ The God who controls everything loves you.

PRAY IT Praise God for being in control of everything. Ask Him to help you make choices that please and honor Him.

DAY 6
GOD IS PERFECT

Verse of the Day: Psalm 18:30

Challenge: Matthew 5:43-48

DO IT Fill in the parts of the eraser that are missing.

How many mistakes have you made this week?

Did you learn anything from your mistakes?

KNOW IT
☐ God is perfect. He does not make mistakes.
☐ God's ways are perfect.
☐ God's teachings are perfect.
☐ God plans for you to be perfect but because you sin, you are not perfect. This is why God's plan was to send Jesus to take the punishment for your sin.
☐ God's plan for your life is to trust Jesus and grow to become more like Him.

PRAY IT Praise God because He is a perfect God. Ask Him to help you follow His perfect plan for your life.

NAMES OF GOD

God is known by many different names in the Bible. Here are some of God's names.

ADONAI	The Lordship Of God	MALACHI 1:6
EL ELYON	The Most High God	GENESIS 14:17-20
EL SHADDAI	God Almighty	PSALM 19:1
ELOHIM	Powerful God	GENESIS 1:1
EL OLAM	The Everlasting God	ISAIAH 40:28-31
JEHOVAH JIREH	The Lord Will Provide	GENESIS 22:13-14
JEHOVAH MEKADESH	The Lord Your Sanctifier*	EXODUS 31:13
JEHOVAH ROPHE	The Lord Our Healer	EXODUS 15:26
JEHOVAH NISSI	The Lord Our Banner	EXODUS 17:15
JEHOVAH ROHI	The Lord My Shepherd	PSALM 23:1
JEHOVAH SABAOTH	The Lord Of Hosts	ISAIAH 6:1-3
JEHOVAH SHALOM	The Lord Is Peace	JUDGES 6:24
JEHOVAH SHAMMAH	The Lord Who Is Present	EZEKIEL 48:35
JEHOVAH TSIDKENU	The Lord Our Righteousness	JEREMIAH 23:6
YAHWEH	I AM	EXODUS 3:14

*Sanctifier means the way God works in your life to help you become more like Jesus.

All of the names of God listed on page 48 come from the Old Testament. The Old Testament was written in the Hebrew language. Check out the letters of the Hebrew alphabet.

Aleph (silent)	Bet b	Vet v	Gimmel g	Dalet d	Hey h	Vav v
Zayin (silent)	Chet ch (or h)	Tet t	Yod y	Kaf k	Khaf kh	Lamed l
Mem m	Nun n	Samekh s	Ayin (silent)	Pey p	Fey ph/f	Tsade ts/tz
	Qof q (ork)	Resh r	Shinl sh/s	Sin s	Tav t	

Practice writing the Hebrew alphabet on a piece of paper.

(Although the alphabet above is written from left to right, the Hebrew alphabet is read and written from right to left.)

HOW AM I CHANGING?

This week you are at the middle of your *Growing in My Faith* journal! Good for you! We have covered a lot of important things. Do you remember these?

- God's plan for your life is for you to become more like Jesus.
- An important way to grow is through regular time alone with God.
- There are different ways of studying the Bible.
- Prayer is talking to and listening to God.
- God is the one true God. There is no one like Him.

Think back to God's plan for you. God's plan for you is to become more like Jesus in your attitudes and your actions. This is a process that will last your whole life, but it also should be happening now. Is it? Let's check and see!

Have you ever had a visit from a relative who hadn't seen you in a while? Maybe one of the first things that relative said to you was something like, "You have changed so much! I can't believe how tall you are!" You may have been surprised to hear this because from day to day you don't notice yourself changing and growing, but your body is always changing, and other people will notice the changes that happen over time.

Growing to be like Jesus can be like that. Sometimes it is hard to notice how you are changing. Sometimes you may need to practice certain things more to grow like Jesus in different areas. This week you will be thinking about yourself. Only you can check your own attitudes and actions and see how you are changing.

Here are some things to think about.
- When you trust Jesus as your Savior and Lord, He becomes the boss of your life.
- Christians still sin, but God forgives us when we confess our sin.
- When we are spending time with God, He helps us want to follow Him.
- When we know we belong to the one true God, we don't have to be afraid.
- Knowing God ourselves makes us want to tell other people about Him.

When you read these statements, do you think they are true about you? Or do you think "I'm not like that at all"? If you think one or more of these statements is nothing like you, that's okay. That is just God showing you something you can work on as you are growing to be like Jesus.

God is at work in the life of every Christian. He is working in your life right now. This week will help you see how He is changing you.

"For it is God who is working in you both to will and to work according to his good purpose." Philippians 2:13

DAY 1
AM I TELLING THE TRUTH ABOUT MY SINS?

Verses of the Day: 1 John 1:8-10

Challenge: James 5:15

 Look for the words SINS, CONFESS, FAITHFUL, FORGIVE, CLEANSE from your Verse of the Day. Be sure you read 1 John 8-10 and then find the hidden words.

J	H	G	F	D	S	A	C
F	A	I	T	H	F	U	L
C	O	N	F	E	S	S	E
B	W	R	E	R	T	Y	A
N	W	S	G	S	R	H	N
B	D	F	L	I	F	H	S
V	S	A	O	N	V	F	E
X	Z	A	U	S	C	E	U

God knows that you will continue to sin, but He has a plan for that, too. Spend time talking and listening to God, asking Him to show you anything you need to confess to Him.

 ☐ We all sin. If we say we don't, we are not being honest. God wants us to tell the truth by confessing our sins (1 John 1:8).

☐ To *confess* means to agree with God. We admit that He is right about our sinful attitudes or actions.

☐ Because we are agreeing with God, we will see our sin as He does. We will hate it and want to turn away from it.

☐ God is always faithful to forgive us when we confess our sin.

☐ God cleanses us when He forgives us. He cleans us so we don't have to keep carrying around our old sins (1 John 1:9).

☐ When you are changing to be like Jesus, you will become more aware of your sins.

 Ask God to show you anything you need to confess. Then confess those sins to God. Ask Him to forgive you. Thank Him for forgiving you.

DAY 2
IS JESUS MY BOSS?

Verse of the Day: John 15:12

Challenge: John 8:12

 Look at the drawings below. Check the ones that show something Jesus has said you must do.

 ☐ Eat ice cream.

 ☐ Obey your parents.

 ☐ Do not judge other people.

 ☐ Ride your bike.

 ☐ Love your enemies.

There are many things in life you have a choice about (eating ice cream, riding your bike), but things that Jesus tells us (obey parents, do not judge, love your enemies) are not optional. Those are His orders to Christians.

 ☐ When Jesus became your Lord, He became the boss of your life.

☐ Following the commands of Jesus makes us grow to be more like Him.

☐ As we grow to be more like Jesus, we will obey Him because He loves us and we love Him.

 Thank God that Jesus is your boss. Ask God to help you know and follow the commands of Jesus.

DAY 3
DO I WANT TO FOLLOW JESUS?

Verse of the Day: Psalm 37:4

Challenge: Proverbs 3:5-8

 DO IT Think of two authority figures in your life (example: mom, dad, teacher, police officer). In the space below, write an example of something they have recently told you to do. Mark an "X" to show whether you WANTED to do it or did NOT WANT to do it.

AUTHORITY	WHAT THEY SAID	WANTED TO DO	DID NOT WANT TO DO
Mom	Clean your room		X

It's always important to obey authorities, but our attitude is important too. You can obey with a "want to" attitude or a "don't want to" attitude.

 KNOW IT ☐ Jesus taught that attitude (what is in our hearts) is as important as our actions (what we do) (Matthew 5:8).
☐ Doing what Jesus tells us may not always be our first choice. Jesus always did what God the Father told Him to do. More than anything He wanted to obey His Father (Matthew 26:39).
☐ One way to tell you are growing as a Christian is that you want to follow Jesus more and more. Is that true about you?

 PRAY IT Thank God for showing you some things Jesus wants. Ask Him to change your heart to help you want to follow Jesus more and more.

DAY 4
AM I AFRAID?

Verse of the Day: Joshua 1:9

Challenge: Isaiah 41:10

 DO IT Read the Verse of the Day if you haven't already. Look at it again. Now use the space to write the things that are commands in this verse.

If we are getting to know God better, we will learn to be less afraid. The verse tells us why we don't have to be afraid. Look at the end of the verse to see the reason we don't have to be afraid. Write the reason here.

 KNOW IT ☐ There are at least 365 places in the Bible where God tells us not to be afraid.
☐ Bad things may still happen to us, but we don't have to be afraid because the all-powerful God is always with us.
☐ It is natural to feel afraid, but the more you trust God, the more your faith grows stronger and your fear grows weaker.
☐ The more you get to know God, the more you will trust Him and the less afraid you will feel. Are you feeling less afraid than you used to?

 PRAY IT Tell God anything that you are afraid of. Ask Him to help you become less afraid. Thank Him for always being with you.

 PARENT Talk Ask your parents to share about a time they were afraid and how God took care of them. Tell your parents about any fears you might have, and pray about them together as a family.

DAY 5
DO I WANT TO KNOW GOD MORE?

Verse of the Day: James 4:8

Challenge: Psalm 86:5

DO IT You've learned some things about God, but there is so much more to know. If you could text God or call Him on the phone, what questions would you like to ask Him? Write some of your questions here.

KNOW IT ☐ There is so much to learn about God. He teaches us about Himself.

☐ The Bible says that Moses talked to God face to face, like a friend (Exodus 33:11). God wants you to know Him and become a friend of His.

☐ When you are becoming like Jesus and getting to know God better, you want to know more and more about God. Is that happening with you?

PRAY IT Thank God for allowing us to know Him. Thank Him for the things you have learned about Him and ask Him to help you learn to know Him better.

DAY 6
DO I WANT TO TELL PEOPLE ABOUT JESUS?

Verses of the Day: Matthew 28:19-20

Challenge: 1 Peter 3:15

DO IT Look at the pictures below. They all show some good news happening. In each yellow circle, write the name of the person you would want to tell if this good news happened to you.

Maybe you would tell certain friends if these things happened to you. Good news is fun to share.

KNOW IT ☐ The best news of all is that Jesus came to earth and died on the cross and rose again.

☐ The word *gospel*, which is the word we use for the story of Jesus, means *good news*. Jesus plans for us to share the good news about Him with the people in our lives.

☐ The more we become like Jesus, the more we want to tell others about Him so they can know Him too. Do you want to tell other people about Jesus? (We will learn more about how to do this later.)

PRAY IT Thank God for the gospel, the good news of Jesus. Ask Him to give you the desire to share the gospel with other people.

THE DISCIPLES OF JESUS

Think about how your life is different since you asked Jesus to be your Savior and Lord. Jesus chose 12 men to follow Him and be His disciples. Read the information about these men. On the journal page 55, write what you hope will be written about you because you followed Jesus.

JOHN was a fisherman on the Sea of Galilee with his father, Zebedee (ZEB uh dee), and his brother James. Jesus called John to be a disciple while he was mending (repairing) nets (Matthew 4:21-22). John helped Peter prepare the Passover meal (Luke 22:8). From the cross, Jesus told John to care for His mother (John 19:26-27).

JUDAS ISCARIOT (joo duhs-iss KAR ih aht) was keeper of the disciples' money bag. Judas betrayed Jesus for 30 pieces of silver (Matthew 26:15).

THOMAS encouraged the disciples to go with Jesus and die with Him (John 11:16). Thomas wanted evidence (proof) that Jesus had risen from the dead (John 20:25). Jesus showed Thomas His hands and side to prove His resurrection (John 20:27).

The Bible tells nothing about **JAMES** except for his name.

THADDAEUS (THAD ee uhs) asked Jesus how He was going to reveal Himself to the disciples and not to the world (John 14:22).

JAMES was a fisherman on the Sea of Galilee (GAL ih lee) with his father, Zebedee, and his brother John. Jesus called James to be a disciple while he was mending nets (Matthew 4:21-22). James was the first discile to be killed for his faith (Acts 12:2).

Jesus called **MATTHEW** to be a disciple while he was a tax collector in Capernaum (kuh PUHR nay uhm). Matthew invited Jesus to a dinner where his friends could meet Jesus (Matthew 9:9-13).

Jesus called **PHILIP** to follow Him as a disciple (John 1:43). Philip found Nathanael (nuh THAN ay uhl) and told him about Jesus (John 1:43-45). Philip went with Andrew to bring some Greeks to Jesus (John 12:20-22).

The Bible tells nothing about **SIMON** except for his name.

ANDREW was a fisherman with his brother Peter on the Sea of Galilee. Jesus called Andrew to be a disciple while he was fishing (Matthew 4:18-20). Andrew brought his brother Peter to Jesus (John 1:40-42), and told Jesus about the boy with the loaves and fishes (John 6:8-9).

BARTHOLOMEW (bahr THAHL uh myoo) or NATHANAEL (nuh THAN nyuhl) was invited to see Jesus by Philip. Jesus called him a "true Israelite" (John 1:45-51).

SIMON PETER was a fisherman with his brother Andrew on the Sea of Galilee. Jesus called Peter to be a disciple while he was fishing (Matthew 4:18-20). Jesus helped Peter to walk on water (Matthew 14:29). Peter denied Jesus before His crucifixion (Luke 22:54-62) and was later forgiven by Jesus (John 21:15-19).

What I hope will be written about me as a follower of Jesus:

Find the disciples' names in the puzzle.

```
J U D A S I S C A R I O T I
O Q W N E R T Y U I O P H J
H B J D V P M N Q W E A A E
N B A R T H O L O M E W D R
Z X M E C I S T B W U S D G
T Y E W U L I H I O A D A S
Q O S T S I M O N P E T E R
A P B X H P O M G J T F U U
Z L A S W E N A J A M E S H
W S J G S T G S T B U G X Y
M A T T H E W X W W G H B N
S X E D C R R F V T G J K L
```

WHAT ABOUT WORSHIP?

You have heard the word *worship*, but do you know what it means? Sometimes we use the word *worship* to talk about a service or a gathering of people that happens at church. That service *can* be worship, but worship is bigger than that. Sometimes we use the word *worship* to talk about music. Music that focuses on God *can* be worship, but worship is bigger than that too.

Maybe this will help. When you hear the word *worship*, think of "worth-ship." Worship is showing or telling God that He is *worthy*. He is worthy of our praise, our honor, and our giving. God is worth giving our lives, and when we respond to Him that way, we worship.

God created you to worship. He wants to have a relationship with you. That's why He sent His Son, Jesus. God wants all people to worship Him, here on earth and forever in heaven.

We worship God when we focus on Him. This means we have time when we give our full attention to God, to who He is, what He has done for us, what He is doing now, and what we know He will do. Giving God our full attention and focusing on who He is can build the attitude of worship in us. An attitude of worship leads to actions.

Worship can take many different forms. One of the most common ways to worship is by singing songs. You probably do this at church. You can do it with your family at home or in the car. You may even do it alone in your room. When we sing songs with words that focus on God and our hearts and minds are focused on Him too, that is worship.

There are other forms of worship. Think about these ways to worship:

- Praying
- Reading or listening to the Bible
- Giving
- Serving others

- Listening to music
- Quietly thinking about God
- Clapping your hands
- Lifting your hands

Worship can happen anywhere. God loves it when Christians meet together to worship, but worship doesn't happen only on Sundays. God also loves it when you worship all by yourself. Worship can be your whole life. As you become more like Jesus, you will become more aware of how worthy God is of your worship.

"Our Lord and our God, you are worthy to receive glory and honor and power, because you have created all things and by your will they exist and were created." Revelation 4:11

DAY 1
WHAT IS WORSHIP?

Verse of the Day: John 4:23

Challenge: Psalm 95:1-7

 DO IT Search your room for three of your most special treasures. Write or draw pictures of the items on the treasure chest.

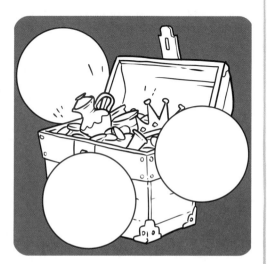

What makes your treasures special? Why are they worth so much to you? Think about God. How much is God worth to you? Is He more special than anything else in your life?

Spend a few minutes thinking about God. Think about how much He loves you, how special He is, and about your relationship with Him.

 KNOW IT ☐ Worship is expressing how important God is to you. ☐ Worship is an action. There are many different ways to worship. ☐ God is worthy of worship. ☐ Worship is focusing on God alone.

 PRAY IT Tell God how special He is and why He is worth so much to you.

DAY 2
WHY SHOULD I WORSHIP?

Verse of the Day: Psalm 96:9

Challenge: Psalm 99:1-5

 DO IT Locate and read these verses in your Bible. Match the verses to the correct descriptions about God.

GOD IS EVERYWHERE	Jeremiah 32:17
GOD NEVER GETS TIRED	Proverbs 30:5
GOD IS ALWAYS FAITHFUL	Psalm 139:7-10
GOD CAN DO ANYTHING	2 Timothy 2:13
GOD IS ALWAYS TRUTHFUL	Isaiah 40:28

Spend time thinking about these characteristics of God. Tell God how thankful you are for who God is. Focus on God, not yourself.

 KNOW IT ☐ The Bible instructs you to worship (Psalm 95:6-7; Matthew 4:9-10). ☐ Worship helps you grow closer to God. ☐ God is the only person worthy of worship. God wants you to worship Him with other people as well as by yourself.

 PRAY IT Close your eyes and sit still. Focus on who God is. Sing songs of praise as your prayer.

DAY 3
WHO SHOULD I WORSHIP?

Verses of the Day: Exodus 20:3-5

Challenge: Psalm 33:1-5

DO IT
CROSS OUT the names ending in the letter R.
CROSS OUT the names of people you play sports or study with. CROSS OUT the names of people you live with. CROSS OUT the names of people elected to leadership positions. CROSS OUT any names with more than three letters.

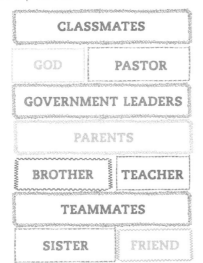

CLASSMATES

GOD   PASTOR

GOVERNMENT LEADERS

PARENTS

BROTHER   TEACHER

TEAMMATES

SISTER   FRIEND

What name is left? This is the only One you should worship.

KNOW IT
☐ God wants you to worship only Him (Exodus 20:3).
☐ Some people believe in more than one god, but there is only one true God (Isaiah 43:10).
☐ God is the Creator of all things. He is worthy of your worship (Revelation 4:11).

PRAY IT
Thank God for the freedom you have to worship Him. Tell God you want to honor Him because He is the one true God.

DAY 4
HOW SHOULD I WORSHIP?

Verse of the Day: Matthew 22:37

Challenge: Psalm 150

DO IT
When you worship, attitude comes before action.

What attitude will lead you to worship? Write your ideas here:

There are many ways to worship. Write down three actions you think of as ways to worship.

1

2

3

KNOW IT
☐ How you worship begins with an attitude that honors God for being worthy.
☐ God wants you to fully mean what you say and do, not just sing songs or go through actions.
☐ The Bible is full of examples of how you can worship. You can sing (Psalm 100:2), pray (1 Thessalonians 5:17), give (Isaiah 58:7), and serve (Matthew 4:10).

PRAY IT
Ask God to help you have the right attitude for worship.

DAY 5
WHEN SHOULD I WORSHIP?

Verse of the Day: Philippians 4:4

Challenge: Daniel 6:1-10

 Use the clock to solve the code.

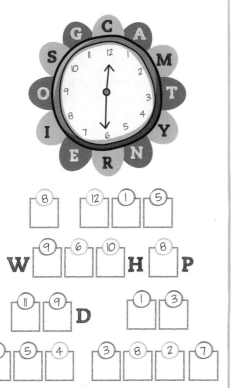

 □ God is not limited by time or place.
□ God wants you to worship Him all the time (morning, noon, afternoon, and evening).
□ God wants the things you do to be a part of your worship of Him. Everything you do should show how important God is to you.

 Thank God that you can worship Him any time.

DAY 6
WHERE SHOULD I WORSHIP?

Verse of the Day: 1 Corinthians 3:16

Challenge: Acts 17:24-25

 Think of where you have been today. Where did you go yesterday? Use the space below to draw pictures of at least three places you have been this week.

Are any of these places you could worship? They all are! You can worship wherever you are. Did you worship at any of these places?

 □ Worship is not limited to a place. You can worship in a church building, school bus, doctor's office, playground, and at home. You can worship *anywhere*.
□ The Bible teaches that your body is God's temple (1 Corinthians 3:16). A *temple* is "a place of worship." Worship doesn't just happen at church. It's a part of who you are!
□ You can worship God privately (Matthew 6:6).
□ You can worship God with other Christians (Hebrews 10:25).

 Ask God to help you worship wherever you are.

 PARENT PAGE:
LEADING YOUR CHILD TO WORSHIP

This page is for your parents to read. Take your journal to your parents and ask them to read this when they have a few minutes.

Parents, from the moment you brought your child home, you have been teaching her. Often you teach with your words or with intentional training, but always you are teaching with your actions. Never doubt that your child learns more from what you do than from what you say.

- Worship is vital in your own relationship with God, and it is vital in your child's relationship with God. How does a child learn to worship? In large part, she will learn from you as you model what worship looks like.

- Many families consistently worship together in their church's worship services. Others may choose for their children to worship in a kids' service. As you decide which option is best for your family, remember that you have the responsibility and the privilege of leading your child to worship. Here are some tips to help you prepare your child to worship.

- Talk with your child about worship. Ask her to define worship. Discuss and expound on your child's definition. Talk about how people worship, the purpose of worship, and how your family worships.

- Make attendance at corporate worship services a priority in your family. Attend services regularly and be on time.

- Show the importance of worship at church by being prepared before Sunday morning. Decide on Saturday what clothes will be worn and have those ready to go.

- Pray with your child before you leave for church.

- If your child attends a separate worship service than the one you attend, be sure to have conversations about that service during the week. Ask questions related to your child's experiences. Find out what music was sung and what was learned from the message. Share your experiences of worship too.

- If your child regularly attends a children's service, you may want to observe the service some Sunday. This will help you have meaningful conversations about your child's experiences.

- If your family worships together, be aware that your child is learning to participate as you model worship. Be sure to actively participate through singing, Bible reading, giving, and praying.

HOW TO TAKE NOTES DURING WORSHIP

Have you ever heard someone say, "Let me write that down so I don't forget it?" How did writing something down help the person recall the information?

Let's see how well you do at remembering. Imagine that your mom asked you and your dad to go to the grocery store. Here's the list of things your mom wants you to buy.

Read over the list three times. You may even say the items out loud. Now, turn your journal over and name the items.

How did you do? Did you remember all the items? What if you had written the items down? Do you think that would have helped you remember it? Try it!

Writing things down helps you remember them better. That is especially important in worship because as we focus on God, we learn the most important things of all. Try to get in the habit of taking notes during worship services. Here are some helps in learning what to write:

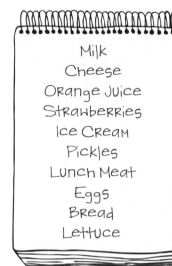

Milk
Cheese
Orange Juice
Strawberries
Ice Cream
Pickles
Lunch Meat
Eggs
Bread
Lettuce

- **Write down key (important) thoughts.** Don't try to write down everything. Summarize what you hear from the pastor or teacher.

- **Write down words you don't understand.** Later you can look them up or ask your parents for help.

- **Don't worry** about correct spelling or writing complete sentences. Your notes are just for you.

- **Write things** in your own words.

- **Practice taking notes.** The more you do it, the easier it will become.

Pages 102-105 provide you with space to take worship notes. Whether you go to a worship service with your family or to a kids' worship service, you can use these pages to help you pay attention and remember what you learned. Take this journal with you to worship. Take notes on what you hear. After the service, respond to the four statements. During the week, look back over your notes. Are you applying the worship notes to your life?

WHAT ABOUT SERVING?

You are one of a kind. There is no one like you! Even if you have a twin who looks like you, you are still two different people. God made each one of us unique. No one else is like you. You are special!

God created you to look the way you look and to have the talents and abilities you have. The reason that God gives us talents and abilities is so we can serve Him. What are some of your talents? Can you sing or run really fast? Can you cook? Can you play a musical instrument or teach people how to do something new? Take a few minutes to think about the gifts God has given you.

Because Jesus is not physically here on earth now, God has another plan for His work to get done here. That plan is *you*! Not only you, of course. God's plan is that all Christians would do His work. That is the purpose of the church.

Sometimes we think of a church as a building, but that's not really right. A *building* can be the place where a church meets, but a church is *people*. The church is made up of Christians who are willing to work together and use their talents and abilities to serve God. God's plan is for every person who is part of a church to serve in some way. There are many different ways to serve. Here are a few:

- Cooking
- Cleaning
- Singing
- Speaking
- Acting
- Teaching

Can you think of some other ways people serve at church?

You may be thinking *I'm just a kid! Can I serve God now, or should I wait until I grow up?* God wants to use you right now! What does it mean to serve God? It means you use whatever abilities you have to help other people know God and learn more about Him. You can help other people sing praises to God. You can use your speaking ability to tell someone about Jesus. God wants every Christian to serve, no matter her age.

The church needs everyone using his gifts and abilities. God will help you learn what He has for you to do. Serving God means doing things to help other people. As a church member, look for ways to do your part. Jesus is our ultimate example of a serving person. When we are serving, we are being like Jesus.

"Serve with a good attitude, as to the Lord and not to people." Ephesians 6:7

DAY 1
JESUS IS MY EXAMPLE

Verses of the Day: John 13: 4-15

Challenge: Mark 10:45

 DO IT Today's "Verses of the Day" seem long because these verses tell an important story. Did you read it? If not, stop now and read. If you need help reading it, ask your parents to read it with you.

Now answer the questions below.

What did Jesus do for the disciples? (v. 4)

Why did He do this? (v. 15)

 The disciples' feet were dirty (and smelly!) but Jesus washed them to set an example for the disciples and all Christians. Because Jesus served others, we should serve others too.

 KNOW IT ☐ Jesus is your example for how you treat other people (John 13:15).
☐ Jesus showed us that He served others.
☐ You follow Jesus' example when you serve other people.
☐ You follow Jesus' example when you obey God in any way, including serving.

 PRAY IT Thank God for the example Jesus gave us. Ask Him to help you become more like Jesus as you use your abilities to serve others.

DAY 2
ONE OF A KIND

Verse of the Day: Ephesians 2:10

Challenge: Psalm 139:13-18

 DO IT Circle the things you are good at doing, or write a new one in the blank space.

SEWING   TEACHING

DANCING   SINGING   DRAWING

PLAYING MUSICAL INSTRUMENTS

PLAYING SPORTS   _____

_____   SPEAKING

How can you use these abilities to serve God and other people?

Think of your family and your good friends. Are any of them exactly like you? What talents and abilities do they have?

If you can't think of what you are good at doing, ask your parents. They will help you.

 KNOW IT ☐ God gave you talents and abilities to serve Him.
☐ Each person has different talents and abilities.
☐ God does not expect you to be perfect when using your gifts, but He does expect you to use them (1 Peter 4:10).

 PRAY IT Thank God for giving you the talents and abilities that you can use to serve Him. Ask Him to help you learn how to use your gifts to help people know more about Him.

 PARENT Talk Talk with your parents about what talents and abilities God has given each of you and how you can use those things for God's glory. Make a plan of one way you can serve others using your talents and abilities this week.

DAY 3
SERVING IN MY CHURCH

Verse of the Day: Ephesians 4:7

Challenge: Ephesians 4:1-7

DO IT Think of two people who help in some way in your church. Draw a picture of each one in a frame below. Under the frame, write their names and what they do for your church.

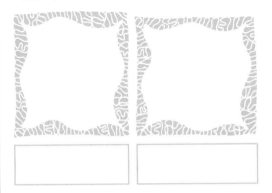

Do these people do the same thing? Probably not, but even if they do, they do their job in a different way. This is how God planned it. He made each one of us unique, but He wants us all to serve in our church. Together we can help more people know God. Think about what you can do in your church.

KNOW IT
☐ God planned for every person in a church to serve.
☐ There are different ways for different people to serve (1 Corinthians 12:4-5).
☐ Besides our natural abilities, God gives Christians gifts to help us show people who Jesus is.

PRAY IT Thank God for all the people who serve in your church. If you don't already help at church, ask God to show you ways to do your part.

DAY 4
SPIRITUAL GIFTS

Verses of the Day: Romans 12:5-8

Challenge: 1 Corinthians 12:27-30

DO IT Every Christian has at least one spiritual gift. This is a gift that helps you use your natural abilities, talents, and opportunities in ways that help people know God. A spiritual gift adds extra meaning to what you do. How do people know their spiritual gifts? Usually people recognize their gifts by noticing what is important to them, what they are passionate about, and what they are good at.

Try this! Turn to pages 66-67. Look at the gifts there and follow the directions. Which gifts do you think God has given you?

KNOW IT
☐ Besides our natural abilities, God gives Christians gifts to help us show people who Jesus is.
☐ The Bible tells us what the spiritual gifts are in Romans 12:5-8 and 1 Corinthians 12:27-30.
☐ When Christians are using their spiritual gifts, other people have the chance to learn more about God.
☐ Sometimes it takes time to recognize what our spiritual gifts are.

PRAY IT Thank God for the spiritual gifts He gives to Christians. Ask Him to help you recognize and use your spiritual gifts.

DAY 5

ATTITUDE CHECK

Verse of the Day: Psalm 100:2

Challenge: Ephesians 6:7-8

 DO IT Number these chores from your least to most favorite.

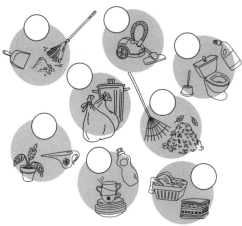

What kind of attitude do you have when doing these chores? What does your attitude say about you? Did you know you are serving God when you are serving your family or other people? You don't have to be at church to use your talents or abilities.

 KNOW IT ☐ God wants you to treat your family members with kindness.

☐ You can use your abilities and gifts to serve people *anywhere* and *anytime*.

☐ We honor Jesus when we follow His example by serving other people.

☐ God wants your actions, attitudes, and words to be pleasing to Him.

 PRAY IT Ask God to help you have a good attitude about serving your family and friends. Ask Him to give you more opportunities to serve.

DAY 6

I'M JUST A KID!

Verse of the Day: 1 Timothy 4:12

Challenge: 1 Timothy 4:11-16

 DO IT What are some things that adults can do but you cannot?

There may be some things that you have to wait to do, but serving God is not one of them. Think about the talents and abilities, and spiritual gifts God has given you. List three of them. Write how you can use your gifts to serve.

TALENTS, ABILITIES, & GIFTS	HOW I CAN USE THESE GIFTS

 KNOW IT ☐ Your church provides ways for you to help other people.

☐ You can find ways to serve outside of church by just noticing where people need help.

☐ You are not too young to use your talents, abilities, and spiritual gifts.

 PRAY IT Ask God to give you opportunities to use your talents, abilities, and gifts.

SPIRITUAL GIFTS

God gives people talents and abilities to use to bring Him glory. God also gives every Christian spiritual gifts to use to serve Him and others.

Look at six of these gifts that God gives Christians. Read the information about the gifts and circle ways you can use these gifts this week. Write in additional ways Christians can use these gifts. Which gifts do you think God has given you?

SERVING

God gives this gift to some Christians to help meet the needs of people or help them do things.

→ Take clothes to a shelter

→ Clean an area of the church

→ Decorate bulletin boards

→ Plant flowers for someone

→ Wash dishes

→ Fold laundry

TEACHING

God gives this gift to some Christians so they can help others learn new things about God.

→ Help a preschooler read a book about God

→ Teach a song about Jesus to someone

→ Tell a Bible story to a group of kids

→ Explain how to spend time with God to a friend

ENCOURAGING

God gives this gift to some Christians so they can say words of comfort to help make others feel better.

→ Write a note or letter to someone

→ Send an e-mail telling someone he did a good job

→ Spend time with an elderly person

→ Say, "Good job" to someone at school

HELPING OTHERS

God gives this gift to some Christians to help people in need.

→ Rake leaves for someone

→ Prepare and deliver food to someone who is sick

→ Spend time talking with someone

→ Make get-well cards for people in the hospital

HOSPITALITY

God gives this gift to some Christians so they can help people feel loved and welcomed.

→ Serve a meal at a homeless shelter

→ Gather and deliver clothing

→ Make gift baskets for new people in the community

ADMINISTRATION

God gives this gift to some Christians so they understand how to get things done.

→ Clean out and organize a storage room

→ Plan a class party

→ Prepare a checklist of items to be completed

WHAT GIFTS DO YOU THINK GOD HAS GIVEN YOU?

*Adapted from Talent Search by Hope Winter, LifeWay Press, ©2000.

WHAT ABOUT GIVING?

When you attend someone's birthday party, what do you take? A gift! At Christmas, what do you give people? Gifts! Everyone likes to receive presents, but why do you give them?

Giving someone a gift is a way of showing you care about him. You might give someone a gift to honor him or to say thank you for doing something special. You might give a gift to show your love for someone.

Think about things you give or receive as gifts. Often gifts are purchased with money, but sometimes they might be homemade. Spending time with someone or sharing your talents can also be gifts. What are some gifts you have given people? How did the gifts make the receiver feel?

We should give gifts to God too. The special word for gifts we give to God is *offering*. Your offering to God might be money you give at church, time you spend serving others, or telling someone about Jesus. Some people are confused when they hear, "Give God your offering," but they do not see God. The money you give at church is used for the various ministries your church provides. Giving your money to the church is the same as giving it to God.

A *tithe* is a special kind of offering where people give one-tenth of all the money they earn to God. God gave the Israelites a law requiring them to give one-tenth of their possessions (the things they own) to Him (Leviticus 27:30,32).

Does God need your gifts? No, He *doesn't* need them! After all, He created everything! So, why should you tithe or give an offering? In the Old Testament, tithing was in response to God's command. As Christians, we tithe in response to God's sacrificial love for us.

We can even give more than a tithe! Giving to God shows that He means more to us than money or the things we own. By bringing an offering to God, you give God glory by honoring and loving Him.

By giving back at least one-tenth of the incredible blessings God has given you, you are glorifying God. As you give, your heart will want to honor God more and more, just like Jesus did.

"Remember the words of the Lord Jesus because he said, 'It is more blessed to give than to receive.'" Acts 20:35b

DAY 1
FIRST THINGS FIRST

Verse of the Day: Proverbs 3:9

Challenge: Psalm 24:1-2

DO IT How many of these items do you own? Put an X over the items you own.

Who gave you these things?

What do these gifts tell you about how people feel about you?

KNOW IT
☐ God gave you the gift of His Son, Jesus, to pay the penalty for your sins. God loves you that much!

☐ You can honor God by giving offerings of money, things you own, or time.

☐ God wants your best, not the time or money you have left over.

☐ Giving to God shows your love and thankfulness for what He does for you.

PRAY IT Ask God to show you how you can honor Him with the things you own.

DAY 2
GOD OWNS IT ALL

Verse of the Day: 1 Chronicles 29:11

Challenge: 1 Chronicles 29:11-14

DO IT Locate the word "one" on the center back of a dollar bill. What words are written above the word? Find a penny, nickel, dime, and quarter. What four words regarding God are on each coin?

KNOW IT
☐ God created everything from nothing.

☐ God owns everything. He does not *need* you to give things back to Him, but He *wants* you to.

☐ God wants people to give offerings to help them show their love and honor to Him.

☐ Giving offerings shows obedience to God.

PRAY IT Thank God for all the many things He has given you. Name some of His gifts to you.

69

DAY 3

CHECK YOUR ATTITUDE

Verses of the Day: 2 Corinthians 9:6-8

Challenge: Philippians 2:5-11

 DO IT   Look at the faces below. Draw a line from each statement to the face that best describes it. You can use a face more than once.

"I just received a gift."

"I need to give my offering."

"Mom says I should tithe on my birthday money."

"I worked for my money. It's all mine!"

What does the Bible say about the type of attitude you should have when you give?

 KNOW IT   ☐ God wants you to give Him your offerings, and He wants you to have a good attitude about giving.
☐ Being a church member brings responsibilities and privileges. One responsibility church members have is to give offerings and tithes.
☐ Becoming like Jesus means being like Him in both our actions and our attitudes. God always knows your attitude.

 PRAY IT   Ask God to help you have a positive, cheerful attitude when giving.

DAY 4

MORE THAN MATH

Verses of the Day: Deuteronomy 14:22-23

Challenge: Leviticus 27:30

 DO IT   Shade in one tenth of the dollar bill and coins.

If you have a dollar bill, one-tenth would equal 10 cents.

 KNOW IT   ☐ A tithe is an offering of one-tenth of your money.
☐ God gave the Israelites a law saying one-tenth of all they had should be set apart as holy and given to God.
☐ Tithing is more than math. It is a way to obey God and honor Him with your possessions.
☐ Tithing reminds you that everything you have comes from God.

 PRAY IT   Ask God to help you understand the importance of tithing. Ask Him to help you remember He gave you all that you have.

DAY 5
A PERSONAL ISSUE

Verse of the Day: Malachi 3:10

Challenge: Mark 12:41-44

 DO IT Write "My Tithe" on an envelope.

 My Tithe

Count the amount of money you have in your bank or wallet. For each dollar you have, place one dime in the envelope. Take your tithe to church with you on Sunday and place the envelope in the offering.

Whenever you receive money as payment for something, set aside one-tenth as an offering to God.

 KNOW IT
☐ God loves you and wants to bless you.

☐ God promises if you are faithful to give Him your tithe, you will be blessed by your giving.

☐ You do not have to tell anyone except your parents how much money you give. That is between you and God.

☐ A tithe is one-tenth, but you can give more than one-tenth.

 PRAY IT Thank God for all the things He gives you. Ask Him to help you be faithful with your tithe.

DAY 6
WHERE IS YOUR TREASURE?

Verse of the Day: Matthew 6:21

Challenge: Matthew 6:19-20

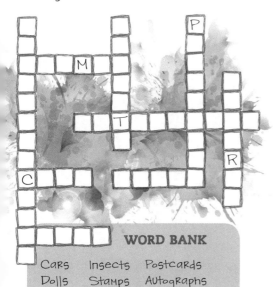

WORD BANK

Cars	Insects	Postcards
Dolls	Stamps	Autographs
Shoes	Tshirts	Baseball cards

 DO IT Write each item in the correct place in the puzzle.

These are all things people collect. Do you collect anything? If so, what?

How valuable is your collection? Where will your collection be in 10 years? 20 years?

 **KNOW IT**
☐ God wants you to keep your priorities in order. Collecting things is OK, but don't let them become the most important part of your life.

☐ God wants you to focus on your relationship with Him.

☐ One day you may get rid of the things you collect, but your relationship with God is forever.

PRAY IT Thank God for your greatest treasure—Jesus.

1. DOWN

Without my offerings, my church would not be able to have a
_____ to meet together for worship and Bible study.

2. ACROSS

Part of my offerings are used to pay our _____ to teach and train
people for ministry.

3. DOWN

The offerings given at my church help people both in the local and global
_____.

4. DOWN

Materials and Bibles are bought for people of all ages to have
_____.

5. DOWN

My offerings help provide _____ for families who cannot afford
to buy it.

6. ACROSS

Without my offerings, our church would not have many of the
_____ we need such as paper, crayons, markers, and glue.

7. DOWN

Have you ever wondered how much the _____ such as lights
and heat cost? My offering helps pay for these things.

8. ACROSS

Part of my offering is used to help people in my town, state, country,
and around the world learn how much Jesus loves them. This is called
supporting _____.

WORD BANK

Bible Studies   Church Staff

Church Building   Community

Utilities

Supplies   Food   Missions

GIVING UP SOMETHING

Imagine that it is the night before you have a big test. You start to study for your test, but you get distracted and start playing a game or watching a show. Before you know it, it's time for bed, and you haven't studied much at all. The next day, you know for sure you made a mistake the night before. You really, really wish you had stayed focused on studying. Has something like this ever happened to you?

It happens to all of us. Even when something like a test is really important to us, something not as important takes our attention away. This happens even when God is the most important thing to us. Other things can take our attention from Him.

The Bible teaches a way to focus on God, especially in times when something big is happening in our lives. The word the Bible uses is *fasting*. Usually in the Bible, *fasting* referred to going without eating for a period of time. Many people did this in Bible times. Moses, David, Paul, and even Jesus fasted. Today, many Christians fast at times to focus on God more. Going without food makes them hungry, of course. That hunger is a reminder to them to focus on who God is.

Because you are still growing and your body needs a steady supply of food, it's not always a good idea for kids to fast by giving up food you need for a long time. But the same idea can work with other things! In order to focus more on God, you can give up something else that is important to you. Going without that important thing will remind you to think about God. It could mean giving up TV, your iPad®, a favorite game, sugary snacks...anything you do or use every day. It needs to be something you will notice you are missing. For now, we will just call it *something*. It works like this:

- You decide to give up *something* you normally do or have. You decide how long the giving up will last.

- You tell God you are giving your *something* up to help you pray or focus on Him. You don't have to tell anyone else.

- You miss your *something*. Every time you miss your *something*, you remember why you are giving it up.

- You focus on God. You think about why He is worth focusing on. You talk to Him.

- The time for your giving up ends. You can have your *something* back. Now you have spent extra time with God. You know Him better and you have grown to be more like Jesus.

This idea may be new to you. That's OK. This week we will look more at what it means to give up something so we can focus more on God.

"Set your mind on things above, not on earthly things."
Colossians 3:2

DAY 1
FASTING

Verse of the Day: Matthew 4:2

Challenge: Matthew 4:1-4

 DO IT
Mad Libs!
(Don't look ahead)

Name any place_____

Name any number _____

Name any food _____

Use your items to fill in the blanks:

Jesus was led into the _____.
(place)

Jesus fasted for _____
days and nights. (number)

Satan tempted Jesus to turn stones into
_____ . (food)

Do your answers make sense? You can look at today's challenge verses (Matthew 4:1-4) to find the correct answers.

 KNOW IT
☐ Before Jesus began His work on earth, He did not eat for forty days and forty nights (Matthew 4:2).

☐ He used this time to pray and prepare to do what God sent Him to do.

☐ Right after this long fasting, Satan came and tempted Jesus to turn stones into bread (Matthew 4:3).

☐ Even though Jesus was so hungry, He did not turn the stones into bread (Matthew 4:4).

☐ God gave Jesus the strength He needed.

☐ Giving up something important can help us to spend more time with God, too.

 PRAY IT
Thank God for the example Jesus gives us. Ask Him to show you if there is something you should give up for a while.

DAY2
NEED OR WANT?

Verse of the Day: Psalm 23:1

Challenge: 1 Timothy 6:17

 DO IT
Look at the list below. Which items are things you need? Mark those with an "N." What about the others? Are those things you want? Mark those with a "W."

WATER

PHONE

FOOD

TV

CANDY

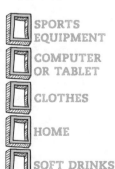
SPORTS EQUIPMENT

COMPUTER OR TABLET

CLOTHES

HOME

SOFT DRINKS

Think through all the things you will use tomorrow. How many are things you need and how many are things you want? Is one of your "want" items something you could give up for a while to help you focus more on God?

 KNOW IT
☐ God gives us everything we need in Jesus (Psalm 23:1).

☐ God gives us many things we want (Matthew 7:11).

☐ Although it is not bad to have things we want instead of need, it is good to know the difference in those things.

 PRAY IT
Thank God for loving you enough to give you everything you need in Jesus and much more.

DAY 3
IT'S ABOUT TIME

Verse of the Day: Matthew 6:33

Challenge: Psalm 1:1-2

DO IT There are 24 hours in every day. If you sleep 10 hours a night, then you have 14 hours to spend every day. How do you spend your time? Look at the circles below. Beside each one, write how many hours you spend on that activity in one day.

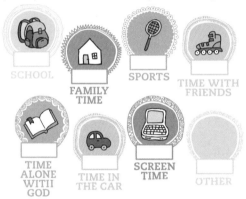

SCHOOL
FAMILY TIME
SPORTS
TIME WITH FRIENDS
TIME ALONE WITH GOD
TIME IN THE CAR
SCREEN TIME
OTHER

What do you think about how you spend your time? Does the way you spend your time show how important God is to you? Is there an activity you could give up for a while to have more time to focus on God?

KNOW IT ☐ God intends for us to have a balance of work and rest in our lives.
☐ How you spend your time determines how you think and feel.
☐ God wants you to spend time thinking about Him.

PRAY IT Ask God to help you know the best way to use your time.

PARENT Talk Discuss with your parents how your family spends their time. Decide how you can use your time to focus more on Jesus.

DAY 4
REFOCUS

Verse of the Day: Psalm 139:2

Challenge: Psalm 19:14

DO IT Let's try it! Just for one day — today or tomorrow — decide to give up something you usually use or something you usually do. Think about it! What will you give up for 24 hours? Write it in the first bubble.

Now it's time to decide what to focus on whenever you miss what you are giving up. You could choose one thing to pray about. Is there something you want to ask God to change in you to be more like Jesus? Something to ask God to do for someone else or for you? What will you pray for? Write it here.

KNOW IT ☐ When you give up something to refocus, missing that object or activity will remind you to pray.
☐ God wants us to pray.
☐ God always answers our prayers. He may answer "Yes," "No," or "Not now."
☐ When we talk to God about something, He often changes our thoughts and our desires.

PRAY IT Ask God to help you in giving up something important to you so you can focus on Him.

DAY 5
TAKING ON

Verse of the Day: Colossians 3:12

Challenge: Isaiah 26:3

DO IT Fill in the blanks below to discover what God is like and what you might be like.

God is **GI▢ING**
Sometimes I am **SE▢FISH**
God is **KI▢D**
Sometimes I am **UN▢IND**
God is **HO▢EST**
Sometimes I am **DIS▢ONEST**
God is **FOR▢IVING**
Sometimes I am **UN▢ORGIVING**

Do you see some things you need to change? Circle one of the things in the "Sometimes I Am" list. Draw an arrow to the opposite word in the "God is" list. Now for the next 24 hours, remember to "give up" the attitude or action in your list, but "take on" the attitude or action in God's list. Every time you remind yourself you have given up being selfish, look for a chance to be giving.

KNOW IT
☐ Because Christians have the power of the Holy Spirit in us, we can decide to give up old behavior and change to new behavior to be more like Jesus.
☐ Practicing this is a way to focus on who God is.
☐ When we focus on becoming more like Jesus, we can be sure God will help us.

PRAY IT Ask God to show you what needs to change in your life and to help you make that change.

DAY 6
ATTITUDE CHECK

Verse of the Day: Isaiah 58:6

Challenge: Isaiah 58:6-12

DO IT Look at the pictures below. Write a description beside each one describing what they are doing or feeling.

Which one of these shows a right attitude for a time of fasting or giving up something to focus on God?

KNOW IT
☐ A time of fasting or giving up something is NOT a way to get God to do what we want.
☐ A time of fasting or giving up something is NOT something to brag about to others.
☐ A time of fasting or giving up something should be done only because we want to know God more.
☐ God describes what a fast should be in Isaiah 58:6-12. A fast should be a time of changing to be and do what God wants us to be and do.

PRAY IT Tell God you are willing to do what He wants you to do. Ask Him to show you ways to please and honor Him.

WHY GIVING UP SOMETHING (FASTING) MAY BE A GOOD IDEA FOR YOU

Only you can decide if it will help you become like Jesus to go through the exercise of giving up something for a short while. As you have seen, many people in the Bible practiced fasting— or giving up food—for a while. Many modern-day Christians also fast sometimes. You too may feel you want to give up something else so you can focus more on God. Take another look at how that works.

1 Now you have spent extra time with God. You know Him better and you have grown to be more like Jesus.

1 You decide to give up something you normally do or have. You decide how long the giving up will last.

2 You tell God you are giving your something up to help you pray or focus on Him. You don't have to tell anyone else.

7 The time for your giving up ends. You can have your something back.

FASTING

6 You focus on God. You think about why He is worth focusing on. You talk to Him.

3 You miss your something.

5 Every time you miss your something, you remember why you are giving it up.

FASTING IN THE BIBLE

In Bible times, many of God's people would fast (go without food for a period of time) so they could focus on God. Who did that? Here are some examples:

MOSES

Moses fasted two times for forty days and forty nights each. At the end of his first fast, God gave him the stone tablets with the 10 Commandments (Deuteronomy 9:9-11). In his anger toward the people who practiced idolatry, Moses broke the tablets. He then fasted again for 40 days and 40 nights, praying for the people (Deuteronomy 9:18-19).

KING JEHOSHAPHAT

King Jehoshaphat announced a fast through all of Judah to pray for the defeat of the enemies of God's people (2 Chronicles 20:3).

DAVID

David fasted to humble himself before God and pray for God's favor (Psalm 69:10).

ANNA

The elderly lady, Anna, saw baby Jesus and recognized He was the Messiah. She had a routine of fasting and praying in the temple. In answer to Anna's prayers, God allowed her to see the Messiah (Luke 2:37).

JESUS

Jesus fasted for 40 days and nights while He was in the desert before beginning His public ministry. Satan tempted Jesus to turn the stones into bread, but Jesus overcame the temptation (Matthew 4:2).

SAUL (PAUL)

After Saul was blinded on the road to Damascus, he did not eat for three days. Following this, Saul became a strong follower of Jesus (Acts 9:9).

CHURCH IN ANTIOCH

These Christians prayed and fasted together. While they were doing this, the Holy Spirit told them to send Saul and Barnabas out for special work (Acts 13:2).

THINK ABOUT OTHER PEOPLE

The Bible tells a story about a day when the religious people tried to trick Jesus by asking Him this question: "What is the greatest commandment?" Perhaps they thought that He would have to pick one of the 10 Commandments as most important and then they would trap Him by asking about the other 9. But no! Jesus was smarter than any of them. He wrapped all the 10 Commandments into 2. This is what He said:

"Love the Lord your God with all your heart and with all your soul and with all your mind. This is the greatest and most important command. The second is like it: Love your neighbor as yourself" (Matthew 22:37-39).

What Jesus meant is that if we do these two things—love God with everything we have and love other people like ourselves—then it will be natural for the things we do to please God.

This week we will talk about loving other people. When Jesus said to love our "neighbor," He didn't mean just our friend who lives next door. "Who is our neighbor?" was the very next question the religious people asked. To answer the question, Jesus told the story of the Good Samaritan (Luke 10:30-37). Jesus was showing them (and us) that He wants us to consider all people as neighbors.

Even when people are different from us, Jesus wants us to show love and kindness to them. This is so important that He says it is "like" the first command, which tells us to love God.

The next time you are at the grocery store, school, or a park, look around at the people. Do all the people look the same? Do they all wear the same types of clothing? Do they all eat the same types of food? God created people unique. Just like people are unique in the way they look, dress, and eat, they are different in what they believe.

Jesus makes it clear His followers are supposed to love all people, no matter how they look, dress, eat, or believe. Whether they know it or not, every person on earth is a person Jesus loves and wants to trust in Him. He loves them the same as He loves you. It is your job to show others that Jesus loves them.

This week we will be thinking about this big job Jesus gave us. Let's think about other people and how we can show love to them.

"Consider others as more important than yourselves."
Philippians 2:3b

DAY 1
LOVE GOD, LOVE PEOPLE

Verses of the Day: Matthew 22:37-39

Challenge: Luke 10:30-37

 DO IT In the first frame below, draw a sketch of someone who is easy for you to like. In the second frame, draw a sketch of someone who is not so easy for you to like.

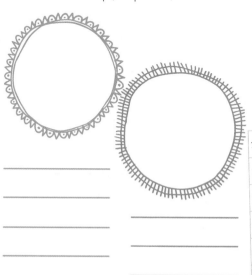

_____

_____

_____   _____

_____   _____

                       _____

Underneath the frames write two ways you could show God's love to each of these people. Which one is harder for you to think of?

 KNOW IT
☐ God showed His love for all people by sending Jesus to die for us (Romans 5:8).

☐ Jesus has commanded us to love other people. Loving them is a way to obey Him (John 14:15).

☐ We can be loving in our actions toward people even before we know them well enough to feel like we love them.

☐ Loving other people is an important way we show our love for God (John 13:34-35).

 PRAY IT Tell God it is not easy for you to love some people. Ask Him to help you show love to them no matter what.

DAY 2
RESPECT

Verse of the Day: 1 Peter 2:17

Challenge: Colossians 3:12-15

 DO IT We usually think of respect as the feeling we have for someone we admire. Who is someone you respect? When we respect people, we care enough about them to think about their feelings before we act. Color in the boxes with a number 1.

1	1	1	2	3	1	1	1	1	5	1	1	1	1	2	1	1	1	9	3	1	1	1	1	7	5	1	1	3	5	1	1	1	1	1
1	5	3	1	4	1	5	3	4	3	1	7	7	1	5	1	3	4	1	2	1	4	7	6	8	1	2	2	1	2	3	4	1	5	6
1	2	6	1	4	1	5	8	2	3	1	8	6	3	7	1	2	3	1	6	1	7	4	0	5	1	0	3	5	8	3	2	1	0	6
1	1	1	7	6	1	1	1	5	8	1	1	1	1	7	1	1	1	7	4	1	1	1	8	2	1	5	4	8	2	7	4	1	5	5
1	1	2	8	8	1	5	8	8	6	4	3	4	1	7	1	2	3	4	5	1	2	0	3	4	1	7	8	6	0	8	4	1	3	7
1	7	1	4	8	1	2	8	5	6	1	7	8	1	7	1	2	3	6	7	1	4	3	2	4	1	6	2	1	7	2	4	1	6	2
1	4	7	1	5	1	1	1	1	4	1	1	1	1	5	1	8	5	8	7	1	1	1	8	4	1	1	7	4	8	4	1	4	6	

 KNOW IT
☐ Respect is how you feel about someone. It can be admiration or understanding they are important.

☐ All people are important to God.

☐ Respect is also how to treat someone. You show respect when you show you care about another person's feelings.

☐ We can respect others and we can respect ourselves. This is why Jesus said, "Love your neighbor as yourself."

☐ The Bible says to "*Consider others as more important than yourselves*" Philippians 2:3b.

 PRAY IT Ask God to help you consider others important and to show respect for them by caring about their feelings.

DAY 3
UPSIDE DOWN

Verse of the Day: Mark 9:35

Challenge: Colossians 3:12-15

 DO IT Which one of these would you say is most important? Number them 1-6, starting with least important to most important.

TEACHER CRYING BABY

KID KING

 SISTER   POLICE

Did you put a 1 beside each picture? People have their own ideas about who is most important. You should always check to be sure your ideas match with what Jesus says. Jesus values all people.

KNOW IT ☐ Jesus said "If anyone wants to be first, he must be last and a servant of all" (Mark 9:35).
☐ Our world values powerful people. Jesus values all people.
☐ Jesus wants His followers to value the least powerful people (Mark 9:37).

PRAY IT Thank God for being a God who values all people. Ask Him to help you do the same.

DAY 4
KNOW WHAT YOU BELIEVE

Verses of the Day: John 8:31-32

Challenge: Acts 17:10-12

 DO IT Sometimes it is a challenge to show love and respect for people who believe differently than we do. It is important to know what you believe. The best way to do that is to know the Bible.

Place a check mark beside the facts that are in the Bible.

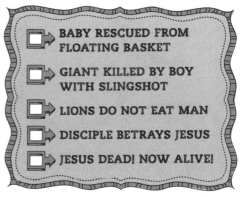

☐ **BABY RESCUED FROM FLOATING BASKET**

☐ **GIANT KILLED BY BOY WITH SLINGSHOT**

☐ **LIONS DO NOT EAT MAN**

☐ **DISCIPLE BETRAYS JESUS**

☐ **JESUS DEAD! NOW ALIVE!**

Did you check all of them? Each of these facts is in the Bible. Knowing and understanding how to find information in the Bible is important. When someone asks you why you believe something you need to be able to locate proof in the Bible.

 KNOW IT ☐ The Bible says there is one true God (Jeremiah 10:10).
☐ The Bible says Jesus is the only way to eternal life (John 14:6).
☐ The Bible says Jesus will return to earth (John 14:1-4).
☐ The Bible says all people have sinned (Romans 3:23).
☐ The Bible teaches being good and working hard will not earn you a place in heaven (Ephesians 2:8-9).

 PRAY IT Ask God to help you learn what the Bible teaches and give you opportunities to share with people who may believe differently.

DAY 5
OTHER BELIEFS

Verse of the Day: Colossians 1:23
Challenge: Philippians 2:9-11

 DO IT Read the list of things some other people believe (page 84).

How does it make you feel to know people believe these things?

Are you concerned that these people do not know the one true God?

Compare the list of things Christians believe (page 85) to what other faiths believe (page 84).

 KNOW IT ☐ God holds each person accountable for what he believes.

☐ God wants Christians to tell the truth about what the Bible teaches and what people should believe.
☐ You can tell people what you believe about God.
☐ You need to know what you believe and how to support your beliefs so when you hear things that are not correct, you can speak up.

 PRAY IT Pray for people who don't know Jesus. Pray for courage to speak the truth to people.

PARENT Talk Talk with your parents about friends your family may have who believe different things. Talk about ways to share the love of Jesus with them.

DAY 6
SHOWING JESUS TO OTHERS

Verse of the Day: Psalm 71:17
Challenge: Isaiah 6:8

 DO IT Draw pictures of you as a baby and now.

In what ways have you changed? Do you like the same foods? What can you do now that you could not do as a baby?

Think about your life since becoming a Christian. Do you know things now that you did not know when you first trusted Jesus as your Savior? Do you pray more? Are you more concerned about other people? If you are following God's plan, you are becoming more and more like Jesus.

KNOW IT ☐ God can use you to help people know the truth about Jesus.
☐ One way to help people know Jesus is to tell them how your became a Christian.
☐ God wants us to tell people about Jesus.

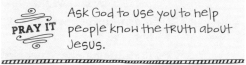 **PRAY IT** Ask God to use you to help people know the truth about Jesus.

HERE ARE SOME THINGS DIFFERENT RELIGIOUS GROUPS BELIEVE.

GOD

- → **Mormons** believe God was once a man, but over time became a god.
- → **Jehovah's Witnesses** believe God is called Jehovah and that He is not Father, Son, and Holy Spirit.
- → **Hindus** believe in many different gods.

JESUS

- → **Jehovah's Witnesses** do not believe Jesus is God. They believe Jesus died on a stake, not a cross, and that Jesus is not coming again.
- → **Mormons** believe Jesus was married and that His death does not provide for the forgiveness of sin.
- → **Islam** followers do not believe Jesus is God's Son or the Savior.

HOLY SPIRIT

- → **Jehovah's Witnesses** do not believe in the Holy Spirit as a one of the Persons of the Trinity (Father, Son, and Holy Spirit).
- → **Mormons** believe the Holy Spirit is not God.
- → **Islam** rejects the idea of the Trinity (Father, Son, and Holy Spirit).
- → **Buddhists** do not believe in the Holy Spirit.

SALVATION

- → **Jehovah's Witnesses** believe you must be baptized as a Jehovah's Witness. They believe you must earn your salvation by the things you do.
- → **Mormons** believe a person is saved through good actions. They believe you cannot have eternal life if you are not a Mormon.
- → **Christian Science** followers do not believe death is real.
- → **Buddhists** believe the goal of life is to be released to nirvana (freedom from the endless cycle of reincarnation).

LIFE AFTER DEATH

- → **Jehovah's Witnesses** believe 144,000 people will become spirits in heaven. The rest of the believers will remain on earth and must live perfect lives for 1,000 years.
- → **Mormons** believe people go to one of three heavens; some people even become gods.
- → **Buddhists** believe people are reincarnated (continue to come back to life until they live good enough lives to be released from this world).

HERE ARE SOME THINGS CHRISTIANS BELIEVE.

 GOD
- → **God** is the one true God.
- → **God** created the world from nothing.
- → **God** loves and values all people.
- → **God** is worthy of praise and worship.
- → **God** is almighty, all-powerful, all-knowing, and always present.
- → **God** is all-eternal, holy, and perfect.

 JESUS
- → **Jesus** is the one and only Son of God.
- → **Jesus** came to earth in human form.
- → **Jesus** lived a perfect life.
- → **Jesus** died to pay the penalty for sin.
- → **Jesus** died on a cross and God raised Him from the dead.
- → **Jesus** will return to earth.

 HOLY SPIRIT
- → **The Holy Spirit** is one of the Persons of the Trinity (Father, Son, and Holy Spirit).
- → **The Holy Spirit** helps people know, understand, and remember all things about God.
- → **The Holy Spirit** inspired Bible writers to know what to write.
- → **The Holy Spirit** helps believers tell people about Jesus.
- → **The Holy Spirit** helps believers grow as Christians.

 SALVATION
- → **Salvation** is a free gift from God.
- → **The punishment** for sin is eternal death and hell.
- → When the **Holy Spirit** convicts people of sin, they can trust Jesus as their personal Savior and Lord.

 LIFE AFTER DEATH
- → **After physical death on earth,** Christians will spend eternity with God
God is all-eternal, holy, and perfect.
- → When **Jesus returns**, all things will be made new.

TELLING OTHERS

What happens when you hear exciting news or something great happens to you? Do you keep the news all to yourself? No—you tell about it! You tell so that everyone knows the amazing thing that's happened.

The truth about Jesus is exciting, fantastic, and amazing news. The gospel is good news, and good news is meant to be shared.

Here are some reasons why it's important for you to tell others about Jesus and the great thing that has happened to change your life.

- God wants you to be involved in His work. God uses people to accomplish His plan. He wants every person to know about Jesus and trust Him as Savior. As Christians tell other people about Jesus, the good news spreads. In Romans 10:14, the Bible asks, "How can people believe if they have not heard about Jesus, and how can they hear unless people are willing to tell?" Your friends and family need to hear about the good news of Jesus. Are you willing to tell them?

- God wants you to follow the example and teachings of Jesus. Jesus spent His time on earth telling people the truth about God and encouraging them to live God's way. Jesus told His disciples to go to all parts of the world and tell everyone about God (Mark 16:15). You can follow Jesus' example and obey His teachings when you tell your friends and family the good news of Jesus.

- God wants you to tell people about Jesus and what He has done for them—and for YOU! That includes telling your friends the truth about God and how Jesus changed your life and can change their lives, too.

So who can you tell? Begin by telling the people closest to you—your family and friends. Next, tell people you see every day at school or in your neighborhood. Then tell people you may not know very well. God wants everyone to hear the good news about Jesus. You can trust God to bring into your life the people who need to hear the gospel from you.

Now you know *why* you need to tell your friends about Jesus. You know *who* you can tell about Jesus. Now discover HOW you can tell your friends about Jesus. As you study this week, you will discover that telling your friends about Jesus is easier than you think. You have good news to share!

"But you will receive power when the Holy Spirit has come on you, and you will be my witnesses in Jerusalem, in all Judea and Samaria, and to the end of the earth." Acts 1:8

Look at the weekly memory verse with your child. This is a good verse for a family challenge. Look on pages 42-43 and choose one way to memorize this verse together.

DAY 1
WHO WILL YOU TELL?

Verses of the Day: Matthew 28:19-20

Challenge: Romans 10:14

 DO IT List the names of six friends. Check whether you think these friends are Christians or not.

My Friends	Christian	
	YES	NO

How do you know if your friends are Christians? If they are not Christians, who will help them know Jesus? Is it you?

 KNOW IT ☐ Many people may act like Christians, but actions do not make a person a Christian. Some people may go to church, but going to church does not make a person a Christian. Only trusting Jesus as Savior and Lord makes a person a Christian.

☐ When you talk with a friend about Jesus, here are some important things to share.

☐ Everyone sins (Romans 3:23).

☐ Sin separates you from God, but He offers forgiveness from sin (Romans 6:23).

☐ God loves you and sent Jesus to die on the cross to pay for your sin (Romans 5:8).

☐ Look on page 90 for more helps on how to share the gospel with your friends!

 PRAY IT Ask God to help you tell your friends about Jesus.

DAY 2
WATCH YOUR WORDS

Verse of the Day: Colossians 4:6

Challenge: 1 Peter 3:15-16

 DO IT Read aloud the following sentence.

May I please have an apple?

Now read the sentence using these different tones of voice:

 angry   sleepy

 sweet   cranky

 whiny   bossy

Which tones of voice would most likely get someone to give you an apple?

When you tell your friends about Jesus, it's not only *what* you say, but *how* you say it that is important.

 KNOW IT ☐ Your actions, not just your words, should tell others what you believe about Jesus.

☐ God loves everyone and wants you to tell your friends about Jesus with kindness and compassion.

☐ When you act like Jesus, your friends will be more likely to listen when you tell them about Jesus.

 PRAY IT Ask God to help your words and actions match what you believe about Him.

DAY 3
BE PREPARED TO TELL YOUR STORY

Verses of the Day: Acts 4:19-20

Challenge: Psalm 107:1

 DO IT Complete page 91. Then fill in the blanks below.

Before becoming a Christian, I ...

I became a Christian when I ...

Now my life is different because ...

Practice telling the story of how you became a Christian and how your life has changed since that time. You could stand in front of a mirror and practice, pretending you are telling your story to a friend. You could practice telling it to your parents. You can use what you wrote above to get started.

 KNOW IT
☐ God wants you to tell your friends about Jesus.
☐ You have a unique story about becoming a Christian.
☐ You can tell a friend about Jesus by sharing what He has done for you.

 PRAY IT Thank God for giving you a story to tell because of Jesus. Ask Him to help you be prepared to tell people what He has done for you.

DAY 4
KNOW HOW TO USE THE BIBLE

Verse of the Day: 2 Timothy 2:15

Challenge: 2 Timothy 3:14-17

 DO IT Find the following verses in your Bible, and bookmark them as you find them.

☐ ROMANS 3:23
☐ ROMANS 6:23
☐ 1 JOHN 1:9
☐ JOHN 3:16
☐ ROMANS 10:13
☐ ACTS 3:19
☐ EPHESIANS 2:8—9

Now close your Bible. Open it again and practice finding the verses.

 KNOW IT
☐ The Bible explains what Jesus did and how a person can become a Christian.
☐ The more you learn about the Bible, the better prepared you will be to talk with your friends about Jesus.
☐ The more you practice finding verses in your Bible, the easier it will become.

 PRAY IT Ask God to help you know how to use the Bible when you tell your friends about Jesus.

DAY 5

TRUST GOD'S POWER

Verse of the Day: Luke 1:37

Challenge: Philippians 4:13

DO IT Use your Bible to match each statement to the correct passage.

GIANT KILLED WITH A SLINGSHOT	Exodus 14:15-29
PETER SET FREE THROUGH PRAYER	I Samuel 17
CROSSED ON DRY LAND	Luke 24:1-12
JESUS RAISED FROM THE DEAD	Acts 12:6-7

What do these Bible stories tell you about God's power? Do you think if God has the power to do these things, He has the power to help you tell your friends about Jesus?

KNOW IT ☐ You can depend on God's power to help you tell your friends about Jesus.

☐ The Holy Spirit helps Christians tell what they know about Jesus.

☐ God loves all people and wants them to hear about Jesus.

☐ You may be afraid to tell about Jesus, but God will give you courage.

PRAY IT Thank God for His power that helps you tell your friends about Jesus.

DAY 6

BE PATIENT. GOD IS IN CONTROL.

Verses of the Day: 2 Peter 3:8-9

Challenge: Hebrews 12:1-2

DO IT Do you like to wait? Why or why not?

Locate a watch or a clock that counts seconds. Start the watch and sit still for 60 seconds.

Was it difficult to sit still? Why?

KNOW IT ☐ God is patient. He wants everyone to know Him and follow Jesus.

☐ God gives all people an opportunity to trust Jesus. Some choose to say "yes" to God, but some choose to say "no."

☐ Your responsibility is to tell people about Jesus, but they must trust Jesus themselves.

☐ The Holy Spirit will help people know when the time is right for them to become Christians.

PRAY IT Thank God that He has the power to do all things. Pray for patience as you tell people about Jesus.

PARENT Talk Read "Sharing the Gospel" together on pages 108-109. Discuss ways you can share the gospel with others.

WHAT DOES THE BIBLE SAY ABOUT BECOMING A CHRISTIAN?

- God loves you (John 3:16).

- Sin is choosing your way instead of God's way. Sin separates people from God (Romans 3:23).

- God sent Jesus so you would not have to die for your sin. Jesus died on the cross, He was buried, and God raised Him from the dead (Romans 5:8).

Becoming a Christian is the most important thing anyone will ever do.

The word gospel means "good news." It is the message about Christ, the kingdom of God, and salvation.

GOD RULES. The Bible tells us God created everything, including you and me, and He is in charge of everything. Invite a volunteer to recite Genesis 1:1 from memory or read it from his Bible. Read Revelation 4:11 and Colossians 1:16-17.

WE SINNED. Since the time of Adam and Eve, everyone has chosen to disobey God (Romans 3:23). The Bible calls this sin. Because God is holy, God cannot be around sin. Sin separates us from God and deserves God's punishment of death (Romans 6:23).

JESUS GIVES. Read John 3:16 aloud. God sent His Son, Jesus, the perfect solution to our sin problem, to rescue us from the punishment we deserve. It's something we, as sinners, could never earn on our own. Jesus alone saves us. Read Ephesians 2:8-9.

GOD PROVIDED. Jesus lived a perfect life, died on the cross for our sins, and rose again. Because Jesus gave up His life for us, we can be welcomed into God's family for eternity. This is the best gift ever! Read Romans 5:8; 2 Corinthians 5:21; or 1 Peter 3:18.

WE RESPOND. We can respond to Jesus. "The ABCs of Becoming a Christian" is a simple tool that helps us remember how to respond when prompted by the Holy Spirit to receive the gift Jesus offers.

The Holy Spirit will help a person know when it is time to become a Christian. If it is not time for your friend to become a Christian, do not push her to do so. God will help her know the right time.

MY STORY

A testimony is a story. When you share your testimony with someone, you are telling him about yourself. Each Christian should be able to tell how she became a Christian. Use these questions to help you write your testimony. Share your testimony with your friends this week.

 I first started thinking about becoming a Christian when...

_____

_____

 To become a Christian, I needed to...

_____

_____

_____

 When I became a Christian, I..

_____

_____

_____

 My life is different since I became a Christian in these ways...

_____

_____

_____

I can help someone become a Christian by...

_____

_____

_____

HOW DO I KEEP FOLLOWING GOD'S PLAN?

When was the last time you played "Follow the Leader" with a group of friends? Was it easy to follow the leader? Why? Did you try to get people to do some difficult tasks when you were the leader? Did the people follow you? How did you feel when your friends did not follow you? How do you think God feels when people do not follow Him?

Following God's plan for your life is not a game. God has a plan for you, and He wants you to follow it. His big plan is for you to become like Jesus. There are other parts to His plan for you that are different from His plan for anyone else. You can trust that God's plan for your life is the best. You may be asking, "How do I follow God's plan for my life?" There are some specific tools you can use when following God's plan seems confusing.

First, you can **read the Bible.** God tells you everything you need to know in the Bible. He wants you to keep Him first in your life, obey your parents, and live in ways that please and honor Him. All the details on how to do these things and more can be found in the Bible. If you're going to follow God's plan, you must learn to dig in to the Bible and learn what it has to say to you. The Bible tells you what God's plan is for your life.

Second, God wants you to **listen to Him.** The world we live in is full of noises and distractions. It is often hard to hear God or even know when God is speaking to you. God will tell you what He wants you to do, so be still and listen to Him.

Third, God lets you **ask Him questions.** If you don't know what to do, talk with God. Ask Him to help you really understand what He's saying to you.

Fourth, **talk to your parents, teachers, or pastor.** You can learn from people who have been following God's plan longer than you have. These people can help you know what to do, and they can answer questions about God's plan.

Remember that following God's plan doesn't mean you will never have problems. Sometimes God allows problems in your life to help you grow and trust Him more. Even in difficult times, ask Jesus to help you follow Him.

In this journal we have talked about some ways you can practice or train to become more like Jesus. Do you remember what these are called? (See pages 10-11.) Being like Jesus is God's BIG plan for your life. The spiritual habits we have talked about are things you will need to keep doing at every stage of your life. Remember that you can always trust God and His plans for you. He will never leave you.

"The Lord is the one who will go before you. He will be with you; he will not leave you or abandon you. Do not be afraid or discouraged." Deuteronomy 31:8

DAY 1
FOLLOW BY LISTENING

Verse of the Day: John 10:27

Challenge: Proverbs 8:32-36

 DO IT Find a quiet place to sit outside if possible. For one minute, close your eyes and listen to everything around you.

LIST HOW MANY DIFFERENT THINGS YOU HEARD

What was the easiest thing for you to hear?

What was the hardest thing for you to hear?

What made it difficult to listen?

 KNOW IT
□ When you belong to Jesus, you will hear and know His voice.

□ Listening sometimes requires you to be still.

□ You can hear God speak through the Bible, prayer, other people, and circumstances.

□ If you have time, review the things you learned in "How Do I Hear God Speak to Me?" on pages 38-41.

 PRAY IT Ask God to allow you to hear Him. Pray for His guidance in following His plans for you.

DAY 2
FOLLOW BY PRAYING

Verses of the Day: 1 Thessalonians 5:16-18

Challenge: Ephesians 6:10-18

 DO IT Finish these common childhood prayers:

Now I lay me down to sleep...

God is great, God is good, let us...

Thank you for the world so sweet, thank you...

What was the very first prayer you learned?

 KNOW IT
□ Prayers like these are good to get you started, but God wants you to move beyond these simple prayers.

□ You can use your own words when you pray.

□ Ask God to show you His plan for your life. He's not keeping a secret that He doesn't want you to know.

□ God will probably not show you everything about your life, but He will show you what you need to know right now.

 PRAY IT Ask God to show you what you should be doing right now.

HOW DO I KEEP FOLLOWING GOD'S PLAN?

DAY 3
FOLLOW BY ASKING

Verses of the Day: Matthew 7:7-8

Challenge: Matthew 6:25-32

 DO IT Ask three different people to give you directions to your school or your church.

What were the people's responses?

Did you get different answers from people even though the question was the same? Why?

Make a list of questions you would like to ask God about your life.

 KNOW IT ☐ People see things differently and as a result, give different responses when asked questions.
☐ The first step to following God's plan is to ask Him to show you what to do.
☐ The Bible tells you to ask God and He will show you (Jeremiah 33:3).

 PRAY IT Read your list of questions to God. Listen as He responds. Thank God for the freedom you have to ask Him questions.

DAY 4
FOLLOW BY FOLLOWING THE LEADER

Verses of the Day: 1 Peter 2:21-25

Challenge: Matthew 6:33-34

RUN IN PLACE FOR **2** MINUTES

TOUCH YOUR TOES **3** TIMES

COMPLETE **10** JUMPING JACKS

 DO IT **Did you do these exercises? Would you have been more motivated to do them if someone was standing in front of you making you do the exercises? Why? What are some things you learned by following someone else's example?**

 KNOW IT ☐ The best way to learn what it means to follow God's plan is to read about the examples Jesus gave you.
☐ Jesus followed God's plan for His life. He left heaven and came to earth just like God planned.
☐ Jesus willingly suffered on the cross, died, and was resurrected to fulfill God's plan for His life.
☐ God knows what is best for you. He has a great plan for you if you will follow the leader—Jesus.

 PRAY IT Thank God for the example Jesus provided. Ask God to help you be obedient like Jesus.

DAY 5

FOLLOW BY DIGGING INTO GOD'S WORD

Verses of the Day: 2 Timothy 3:16-17

Challenge: Matthew 13:18-23

 DO IT Search for tools used for digging and drilling.

E	F	S	P	A	D	E	G
W	A	F	H	G	H	N	D
N	R	H	R	O	K	B	R
L	A	E	P	P	V	V	I
E	K	I	N	I	C	E	L
Z	E	S	A	C	S	Y	L
Q	B	A	C	K	H	O	E

WORD BANK:

Backhoe, Drill, Pick, Rake, Shovel, Spade

Think about tools you use to help you dig deeper into the Bible. You can use Bible dictionaries, concordances, and maps to help you learn more about the events in the Bible.

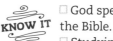 **KNOW IT**
☐ God speaks through the Bible.
☐ Studying the Bible can help you discover God's plan for your life.
☐ The more you study, the clearer God's plan for your life becomes.

 PRAY IT Ask God to help you build a habit of studying His Word each day.

DAY 6

KEEP GOING

Verses of the Day: Philippians 3:13-14

Challenge: Hebrews 10:35-36

 DO IT What is the farthest distance you have ever run or walked? Did you get tired and want to quit? If you were tired but kept going, you pressed on!

Turn back in your journal to page 7. Look at the top of the page. What is the date you wrote there?

That is the first day you started working in your journal. Today is your last day of working in the journal. Write today's date here.

Congratulations!

You may have wanted to quit sometimes, but you kept on until you finished. You kept going!

 KNOW IT
☐ Walking in God's will and following His plan is what He wants you to do for the rest of your life.
☐ You may get tired and be tempted to look back at where you came from. You may wish to stop following God's plan, but don't! Keep going! Keep pressing on!
☐ No matter what happens, God promises that He will always be with you. Keep following and trusting Him!

 PRAY IT Ask God to help you follow His plan even when things get difficult and you want to quit.

THE BIBLE CAN HELP ME WHEN I AM...

ANGRY

Psalm 4:4

Proverbs 15:1

Proverbs 29:22

Matthew 5:21-26

Ephesians 4:26

AFRAID

Matthew 6:25-34

Matthew 10:19

Philippians 4:6,19

FEELING BAD ABOUT HURTING SOMEONE

Proverbs 17:17

Luke 6:37

DISCOURAGED

1 Chronicles 22:13

Romans 8:28

FEELING GUILTY ABOUT SOMETHING I DID

Psalm 32:5

1 John 1:9

FEELING GREEDY

Ecclesiastes 5:10

Hebrews 13:5

HAVING PROBLEMS WITH MY PARENTS

Ephesians 6:1-3

Colossians 3:20

SAD

Psalm 55:22

John 14:27

1 Peter 5:7

WORRIED

Deuteronomy 31:8

Joshua 1:9

Psalm 27:1

Psalm 56:3

Psalm 118:6

Isaiah 41:10

Hebrews 13:6

SICK

Exodus 15:26

Jeremiah 17:14

TEMPTED TO GET BACK AT SOMEONE WHO HURT ME

Leviticus 19:18

1 Peter 3:9

1 Thessalonians 5:15

Proverbs 24:29

TEMPTED TO LIE

Leviticus 19:11

Psalm 34:13

Matthew 19:18

Colossians 3:9

TEMPTED

Matthew 26:41

1 Corinthians 10:13

NEEDING TO KNOW GOD'S WILL

Proverbs 3:5-6

Jeremiah 29:11

Matthew 6:31

TEMPTED TO BE SELFISH

Psalm 119:36

Philippians 2:3

1 John 4:7-8

IT'S TIME TO DISCOVER SOME FUN STUFF ABOUT THE BIBLE. SHARE THESE FACTS WITH YOUR FAMILY AND FRIENDS.

The only nuts mentioned in the Bible are ALMONDS and PISTACHIOS.

THE L O N G E S T CHAPTER IN THE BIBLE IS PSALM 119.

John 3:16 is one of the most memorized verses in the Bible.

Ruth (ROOTH) and Esther (ESS tuhr) are the only books in the Bible named for women.

The Bible contains 1,189 chapters. The shortest chapter in the Bible is Psalm 117. The longest verse in the Bible is Esther 8:9. The shortest verse in the Bible is John 11:35.

Dogs are mentioned in the Bible, but cats are not.

The most frequently named animal in the Bible is the sheep.

THE AVERAGE READER CAN READ THE WHOLE BIBLE IN ABOUT 70 HOURS.

In the King James Version of the Bible, Ezra (EZ ruh) 7:21 contains all of the letters of the English alphabet except one. The letter "J" is not used.

THE TALLEST MAN IN THE BIBLE WAS GOLIATH (GUH LIGH UHTH). HE WAS 9 FEET 9 INCHES TALL.

The word **BIBLE** does not appear in the Bible. Bible comes from the Greek word Biblia, meaning "books."

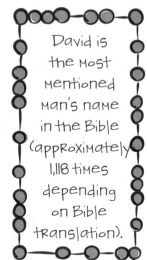

David is the most mentioned man's name in the Bible (approximately 1,118 times depending on Bible translation).

The books of the Bible did not have chapter or verse numbers when they were written.

THE LONGEST NAME IN THE BIBLE IS **MAHERSHALALHASHBAZ**

(may hehr-shal al-HASH baz) (Isaiah 8:1).

Two men, Enoch (EE nuhk) and Elijah (ih LIGH juh) never died. God took them to heaven.

METHUSELAH (MIH THOOZ UH LUH) WAS THE OLDEST MAN IN THE BIBLE. HE LIVED TO BE 969 YEARS OLD.

A DONKEY ACTUALLY TALKED IN NUMBERS 22:28—30.

THE WORD CHRISTIAN ONLY APPEARS THREE TIMES IN THE BIBLE (ACTS 11:26, 26:28, 1 PETER 4:16).

The Old Testament was written in Hebrew (HE broo) and Aramic (ar uh MAY ihk). The New Testament was written in Greek.

1

Therefore, be imitators of God, as dearly loved children, and walk in love, as Christ also loved us and gave himself for us.

Ephesians 5:1-2a

2

But grow in the grace and knowledge of our Lord and Savior Jesus Christ. To him be the glory both now and to the day of eternity.

2 Peter 3:18

3

I have treasured your word in my heart so that I may not sin against you.

Psalm 119:11

4

Help me understand your instruction and I will obey it and follow it with all my heart.

Psalm 119:34

5

Rejoice always; pray constantly; give thanks in everything; for this is God's will for you in Christ Jesus.

1 Thessalonians 5:17

6

My sheep hear my voice. I know them and they follow me.

John 10:27

7

Know that the Lord your God is God.

Deuteronomy 7:9a

9

Our Lord and our God, you are worthy to receive glory and honor and power, because you have created all things and by your will they exist and were created.

Revelation 4:11

10

Serve with a good attitude, as to the Lord and not to people.
Ephesians 6:7

11

Remember the words of the Lord Jesus because he said, "It is more blessed to give than to receive."

Acts 20:35b

8

For it is God who is working in you both to will and to work according to his good purpose.

Philippians 2:13

14

But you will receive power when the Holy Spirit has come on you, and you will be my witnesses in Jerusalem, in all Judea and Samaria, and to the end of the earth.

Acts 1:8

13

Set your mind on things above, not on earthly things. Consider others as more important than yourselves.

Philippians 2:3b

12

Set your mind on things above, not on earthly things. Colossians 3:2

15

The Lord is the one who will go before you. He will be with you; he will not leave you or abandon you. Do not be afraid or discouraged.

Deuteronomy 31:8

WORSHIP NOTES

WHO IS TEACHING?

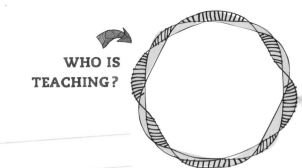

BOOK: _____

CHAPTER: _____

VERSE: _____

Things My pastor/teacher said:

Something I learned about God today:

Something I can do this week Related to what I learned or heard in worship:

Something I can talk with My family about Related to what I learned or heard in worship:

WHO IS TEACHING?

BOOK: _____

CHAPTER: _____

VERSE: _____

...hings my pastor/teacher said:

Something I learned about God today:

Something I can do this week related to what I learned or heard in worship:

Something I can talk with my family about related to what I learned or heard in worship:

WORSHIP NOTES

WHO IS TEACHING?

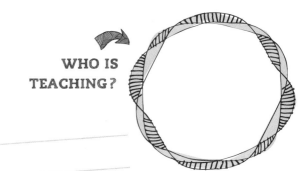

BOOK: _____

CHAPTER: _____

VERSE: _____

Things My pastoR/teacher said:

Something I learned about God today:

Something I can do this week Related to what I learned oR heard in woRship:

Something I can talk with My family about Related to what I learned oR heard in woRship:

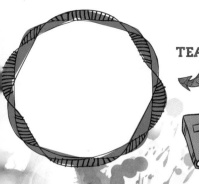

WHO IS TEACHING?

BOOK: _____

CHAPTER: _____

VERSE: _____

...ings My pastor/teacher said:

Something I learned about God today:

Something I can do this week Related to what I learned or heard in worship:

Something I can talk with My family about Related to what I learned or heard in worship:

How do I keep following God's plan and becoming more like Jesus?

Congratulations! You completed your Growing in My Faith journal. So now what?

Think about some of the things you learned. You have studied the Bible, completed the activities, prayed, and thought through new ideas. Have you grown closer to God? Are you becoming more like Jesus?

God wants you to keep growing! Here are some suggestions to help you follow God's plan.

☆ Attend Bible study at your church.

☆ Participate in worship services.

☆ Spend time alone with God.

☆ Read and study your Bible daily.

☆ Pray.

☆ Tell the truth about your sin — to God and to yourself.

☆ Memorize Bible verses.

☆ Tell your friends what you know about God.

☆ Show respect for all people.

☆ Focus on God.

☆ Ask questions when you do not understand things.

☆ Be open to God doing amazing things in your life.

Can you add some other ways to the list?

FOLLOWING UP WITH YOUR CHILD

Your child has completed the *Growing in My Faith* journal. You should be proud! This is a big accomplishment—for both of you. Thank you for being a parent who encourages your child in spiritual growth.

Please do not see the completion of the journal as a final step in growing closer to God. This is just the beginning! The journey continues, and God has given you the privilege of leading your child on a faith journey to becoming like Jesus.

Here are a few suggestions for helping your child continue to grow as a Christian

☆ Set an example for your child as you grow in your own relationship with God.

☆ Model Christ-like characteristics.

☆ Affirm your child when he displays attitudes and/or actions which are like Jesus.

☆ Pray for and with your child regularly.

☆ Look for opportunities to serve in your church and to minister to other people as a family.

☆ Let your child know you place high priority on sharing the gospel with others.

☆ Help your child use his gifts and abilities to serve God and others.

☆ Make it a regular, natural practice to discuss spiritual matters in your daily family life.

☆ Ensure your child participates regularly in Bible study times and worship.

☆ Find times to participate in corporate worship as a family.

☆ Ensure your child is receiving true Biblical teaching.

FIRST THINGS FIRST: WHAT IS THE GOSPEL?

The gospel is the good news that God sent His Son Jesus to die for sinners. God made us and loves us, but we have a problem. We sin. We do not want what God wants, and our sin keeps us from knowing God. Jesus came to earth to pay the penalty for our sin. All who trust in Jesus are freely and fully forgiven of their sin and will live with God forever.

WHO SAVES PEOPLE?

God saves people. As you share the gospel, it is not your job to convince people that you are right about Jesus. Instead, share the good news out of love for God and love for people. Pray that whomever you are talking to would hear the truth and believe.

STARTING POINTS

You can share the gospel from many starting points.

GOD, OUR CREATOR
Ask the person to consider what God has made: the oceans, the mountains, the stars, and more. Talk about how God, who made everything, loves us and wants a relationship with us. However, we cannot have a relationship with Him because of our sin. That's why Jesus came. Explain the rest of the gospel message. Ask, "Do you believe this too?"

HUMANITY
Ask your friend to consider how humans are unique, or special. Talk about how we are so special that God wants to have a relationship with us. However, we cannot have a relationship with Him because of our sin. That's why Jesus came. Explain the rest of the gospel message. Ask, "Do you believe this too?"

JESUS
Ask your friend if she has ever heard of Jesus. What does she know about Him? What does she think about Him? Tell her why Jesus came to earth and explain the rest of the gospel message. Ask, "Do you believe this too?"

YOURSELF
Tell your friend how you became a Christian. Tell him what you believe is true about Jesus, and explain the gospel message. Tell him what is different about your life because you follow Jesus. Ask, "Do you believe this too?"

EXAMPLES FROM THE BIBLE

Read the following stories of Jesus' disciples sharing the good news with others. Choose one story and consider the Who, When, What, How, and Why of it.

★ Peter and the Jews (Acts 2:22-41)
★ Philip and the Ethiopian (Acts 8:26-40)
★ Paul and Barnabas (Acts 14:8-22)
★ Paul in Athens (Acts 17:16-34)
★ Paul before the king (Acts 26:12-29)

DON'T FORGET TO PRAY

Before, during, and after sharing the gospel, it's important to pray. Below is a list of things you can pray for. Can you think of any others?

★ People to share with
★ Opportunities to share
★ Courage and boldness to share
★ Grace and love when sharing
★ The right words when sharing
★ For God to save people

Remember that everyone who hears the good news does not become a Christian right away. That's OK! God saves people according to His perfect plan. You can simply keep praying, loving, and telling others about Jesus.

TIME TO PRACTICE

Practice sharing the gospel with a parent or family member. Remember what you learned in "First Things First" and try to use one of the "Starting Points."

STUDY **1** BIBLE BOOK.

WHO wrote the book and when was the book written?

WHAT is the book about?

WHAT does the book say about God?

HOW did the people act toward God?

WHAT people does the book tell about?

WHAT can you learn about God from the book?

STUDY **1** BIBLE VERSE.

READ
the verse from different Bible translations.

WHAT
are the important words in the verse?

WHAT
are the words you don't understand?

WRITE
the verse in your own words. What can you learn from the verse?

STUDY **1** PERSON.

WHEN
and where did the person live?

WHAT
took place in the person's life?

HOW
did the person act?

WHAT
can you learn from the person?

111

THE GOSPEL:
God's Plan for Me

The word gospel means "good news." It is the message about Christ, the kingdom of God, and salvation.

 GOD RULES. The Bible tells us God created everything, including you and me, and He is in charge of everything. Invite a volunteer to recite Genesis 1:1 from memory or read it from his Bible. Read Revelation 4:11 and Colossians 1:16-17.

 WE SINNED. Since the time of Adam and Eve, everyone has chosen to disobey God (Romans 3:23). The Bible calls this sin. Because God is holy, God cannot be around sin. Sin separates us from God and deserves God's punishment of death (Romans 6:23).

 JESUS GIVES. Read John 3:16 aloud. God sent His Son, Jesus, the perfect solution to our sin problem, to rescue us from the punishment we deserve. It's something we, as sinners, could never earn on our own. Jesus alone saves us. Read Ephesians 2:8-9.

 GOD PROVIDED. Jesus lived a perfect life, died on the cross for our sins, and rose again. Because Jesus gave up His life for us, we can be welcomed into God's family for eternity. This is the best gift ever! Read Romans 5:8; 2 Corinthians 5:21; or 1 Peter 3:18.

 WE RESPOND. We can respond to Jesus. "The ABCs of Becoming a Christian" is a simple tool that helps us remember how to respond when prompted by the Holy Spirit to receive the gift Jesus offers.

ADMIT to God that you are a sinner. The first people God created chose to sin and disobey God. Ever since then, all people have chosen to sin and disobey (Romans 3:23). Tell God you messed up and you are sorry for doing your own thing and turning away from Him through your thoughts, words, and actions. Repent, turn away from your sin (Acts 3:19; 1 John 1:9). Repent doesn't just mean turning from doing bad things to doing good things. It means turning from sin and even from your own good works and turning to Jesus, trusting only in Him to save you.

BELIEVE that Jesus is God's Son and receive God's gift of forgiveness from sin. You must believe that only Jesus can save you and you cannot save yourself from your sin problem—not even by praying to God, going to church, or reading your Bible. Your faith or your trust is only in Jesus and what He did for you through His life, death, and resurrection (Acts 16:31; Acts 4:12; John 14:6; Ephesians 2:8-9).

CONFESS your faith in Jesus Christ as Savior and Lord. Tell God and tell others what you believe. If Jesus is your Savior, you are trusting only in Him to save you. Jesus is also Lord, which means He is in charge and calling the shots in your life. You can start following Him and doing what He says in the Bible. You are born again into a new life and look forward to being with God forever (Romans 10:9-10,13).